natural English

upper-intermediate workbook with key
Lyn Scott & David Scott

OXFORD
UNIVERSITY PRESS

contents

one

start off

natural English showing impatience

1 Dorota is a company manager. She's having a bad day at work! Put these sentences into the conversations below.

a Oh, no! They're hopeless! Can we try a different company?

b ~~For goodness sake! He's giving the presentation. He has to come.~~

c Oh, really! She hasn't been on time once this week!

d Not again. There's always something wrong with it!

e Oh, for goodness sake! He only put in the order on Monday. He knows that it can take up to two weeks.

f Oh, honestly! I asked you to take them yourself. They're urgent.

Karol	Adam just called. He can't come to the meeting this afternoon.	
Dorota	*b*	
1 Dorota	Did you deliver the documents to Head Office?	
Marcus	I sent them this morning.	
Dorota	___	
2 Ingrid	The photocopier's broken down!	
Dorota	___	
3 Robert	Karen's just called. She's going to be late again.	
Dorota	___	
4 Dorota	Did you order some more stationery?	
Marcus	Yes, but they can't deliver it until Thursday.	
Dorota	___	
5 Ingrid	Luca Martini called. He hasn't received his order yet.	
Dorota	___	

say it!

Say it, don't write it! You manage an office. Respond when a staff member tells you these things.

Mr Tanaka wants your monthly report by 2.00 p.m. today.
Manolo called. He's sick. He's not coming in today.
I can't find those documents that you wanted.
The computers aren't working.
The electrician won't be able to fix the air-conditioning until tomorrow afternoon.

> Oh honestly! He knows I haven't got time to do it today.

would you pass the fitness test?

natural English talking about activities

2 Write sentences with the same meaning. Use the words given.

I sometimes have to do some work at the weekends. (bit)
I sometimes have to do a bit of work at the weekends.

1 Do you play sport often? (lot)

_____ ?

2 We only watch a little TV. (much)

_____ .

3 He does no exercise. (at all)

_____ .

4 We often go skiing in the winter. (lot)

_____ .

5 I've only done a little revision for my exams. (much)

_____ .

natural English describing difficulty

3 Some students are talking about an English test that they have just done. Order the words to make sentences.

found / the reading test / I / easy
I found the reading test easy.

1 it / hard / understand / I found / to / the listening test

_____ .

2 the vocabulary test / found / tricky / I / quite

_____ .

3 part / the pictures / hardest / Describing / was / the

_____ .

4 hopeless / I / the grammar test / at / was

_____ .

5 quite / the writing test / found / challenging / I

_____ .

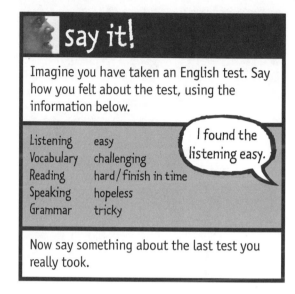

say it!

Imagine you have taken an English test. Say how you felt about the test, using the information below.

Listening	easy
Vocabulary	challenging
Reading	hard / finish in time
Speaking	hopeless
Grammar	tricky

I found the listening easy.

Now say something about the last test you really took.

wordbooster

collocation in dictionaries

4 Underline words that collocate. One, two, or three may be correct.

to look up	homework
	<u>a phone number</u>
	<u>a word</u>

1 flick through	a magazine
	a grammar book
	a computer

2 the latest	news
	fashion
	technology

3 _____ by heart	know
	read
	learn

4 to skip	a few pages
	a class
	lunch

5 _____ the gist	have
	know
	get

Now cover the words on the right and try to remember the collocations.

sporting collocations

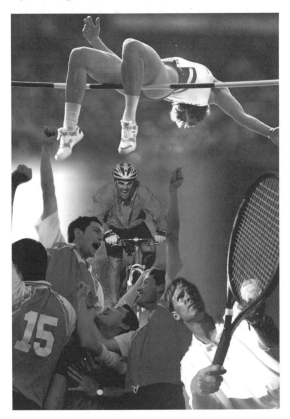

think back!

Remember sporting words that collocate with: take part in / join / win / lose / practise / do / go / go in for

5 Complete the sentences with a suitable verb in the correct form. You can use the same verb more than once.

How long have you been *doing* aerobics?

1 He's _____ skiing next week.

2 I only _____ in for the competition for fun. I can't believe I won!

3 Why don't you _____ a club?

4 You should _____ your technique more if you really want to win.

5 He had never _____ part in a championship before winning this one.

6 Her brother _____ a silver medal at the last Olympic Games.

7 He's very good. How long ago did he _____ the team?

8 My sister _____ karate. She's quite good at it.

grammar *-ing* form and infinitive

6 Isabel is living and working abroad for a year. She has written to a friend. Read her e-mail and underline the correct form.

---

from: Isabel **subject:**
sent: Friday, June 21, 2002 5:02 pm

Hi Alicia! Thanks for your last e-mail. I really enjoyed <u>hearing</u> / to hear all the gossip from home. It cheered me up a lot. I'm enjoying myself but [1] living / to live here is much more difficult than I expected. People do things very differently and I keep [2] doing / to do the wrong thing. The hours are so different here. I can't get used to [3] having / have dinner so early in the evening. Also, instead of [4] having / to have a siesta after lunch, we have to go straight back to work so I'm always tired in the afternoons.

I like my job but if you're not willing [5] working / to work overtime, the boss doesn't like it. I don't mind [6] working / to work late once or even twice a week but he expects everyone to stay late most nights. I'm prepared [7] staying / to stay here for the rest of the year, though, because it's not worth [8] looking / to look for a new job now.

Anyway, sorry to sound so negative! There are lots of things I really like here. I've met some great people and there's a lot to do. I've taken up [9] jogging / to jog and go every morning with my flatmate. She's in really good shape but I tend [10] giving up / to give up after five minutes! I used to [11] running / run three kilometres every day when I was younger but now I'm hopeless!

I'm looking forward to [12] getting / get the photos you said you'd sent. By the way, I've tried to call you a few times but you're never home! What's a good time to ring?

Love
Isabel

---

7 Read Alicia's reply. Complete the text using the verbs in brackets in the correct form (*-ing* or infinitive).

---

from: Alicia **subject:**
sent: Tuesday, June 25, 2002 10:35 am

Hi Isabel

Thanks for your e-mail. Glad to hear that you're having a good time there. I'm really busy! I've just moved into a new flat with a friend of mine, Rosanna. You might remember *meeting* (meet) her at my party last year. I've got my law exams next month, so I'm going to have to stop [1] _____ (work) at the café! I really regret [2] _____ (not study) a bit harder last year. I've been trying [3] _____ (do) at least three hours' work every evening but it's hard. I've also fallen out with Marco. He thought he saw me on a date with another guy but it wasn't like that at all! I bumped into an old friend on the way home from college and we stopped [4] _____ (have) a coffee – that's all!

Please remember [5] _____ (say) hello to Marcello for me.

Love

Alicia

PS Here's my new phone number – 749162. Try calling me after 9.00 p.m. I'm usually home by then!

expand your grammar

get used to / be used to

When something is difficult or unfamiliar at first but it becomes more familiar, or you become accustomed to it, you can use the structure *get used to* sth / *get used to doing* sth.

I didn't like my haircut to start with. I thought it was too short, but now <u>I'm getting used to</u> it.

When I moved to London it took me a long time <u>to get used to living</u> in such a big city.

When you are familiar with something you can use *be used to* sth / *be used to doing* sth.

Our apartment is very close to the airport. When we first moved in I noticed every plane that went overhead, but now <u>I'm used to</u> the noise. In fact, I don't even notice it any more.

In my new job I start work early, at 7.30 a.m. For the first few weeks it was really hard but now <u>I'm used to getting up</u> early. In fact I quite like it because we finish at 3.30 p.m.

You can also use *be used to* sth / *be used to doing* sth in the past.

When I first moved into my own flat it was hard at first because <u>I was used to living</u> at home with my mum.

When we went hiking in the mountains I got very tired because <u>I wasn't used to walking</u> so far.

Replace the underlined words. Use *be used to* or *get used to* in the appropriate form.

When I got here I was freezing all the time but now <u>I'm becoming accustomed to it</u>. And I've bought some warm clothes!
   I'm getting used to it.

1 To start with I found the food too spicy, but now <u>it's OK</u>. In fact, I quite like it.

_____

2 Now <u>I'm becoming more familiar with the money</u>, but when we first got here I kept giving everyone the wrong notes.

_____

3 I found the job quite hard at first because <u>I wasn't familiar with working</u> such long hours.

_____

4 My dad found retirement difficult – he didn't know what to do with himself. <u>He was accustomed to a busy work schedule</u>.

_____

5 When you go abroad, it can often take three or four days <u>to become familiar with the time difference</u> between countries.

_____

say it!

Imagine you are studying or working in England. Say how familiar you are with the things below. Use *be used to / get used to* and the words given.

At first I found it really cold, but now I'm getting used to it.

the weather (cold)
English food (boring)
the accent (strange)
driving on the left (difficult)

learning

grammar wishes and regrets

8 Complete the sentences. Use the verbs in brackets in the correct form.

Your **wishes** and **regrets**

Is there something you would like to change about yourself or your life past or present?

- I'm very shy. I hate going to parties if I don't know everyone there. So I wish I *was* (be) more outgoing.

- I'm retired now and I'm enjoying life but I wish I *hadn't worked* (not /work) so hard. I regret *not spending* (not spend) more time with my family.

- I wish I ¹ _____ (can) sing. I don't want to be a pop star, but I'd like to have a nice voice.

- I really hate the job I'm doing at the moment. In fact I wish I ² _____ (not / have to) work at all.

- I got married when I was 19. It didn't work out and we got divorced after five years. I think we were too young. I don't regret ³ _____ (get) married but I wish we ⁴ _____ (meet) when we were both a bit older – maybe then we would still be together.

- I don't like wearing glasses or contact lenses. I wish I ⁵ _____ (have) perfect eyesight. I suppose I could have a laser operation but I don't like the idea of that.

- I wish I ⁶ _____ (travel) when I was younger but it wasn't as easy in those days. I tell my granddaughter that she should go and see as much of the world as she can.

- There are lots of things about myself I'd like to change, but if I had to choose just one, I'd say I wish I ⁷ _____ (be) shorter. I'm even taller than my boyfriend!

- I left school when I was 16. I really didn't enjoy school and I just wanted to get a job. Now I wish I ⁸ _____ (stay) at school and maybe gone to university. I really regret ⁹ _____ (not get) better qualifications.

- A few years ago I was offered a job abroad. My boyfriend didn't want me to go so I turned down the offer. I wish I ¹⁰ _____ (accept) it because we broke up six months later!

write it!

Write two paragraphs about yourself. What would you like to change about yourself now? What regrets do you have about the past?

natural English describing your language ability

9 How well can these people speak German? Order the sentences.

- a I can get by in German.
- b I speak German quite well, but it's a bit rusty.
- c I'm fluent in German.
- d I only know a few words of German.
- e I wish I could speak German.

5 ☐ ... *speaks it very well*
4 ☐
3 ☐
2 ☐
doesn't speak it at all ... 1 [e]

vocabulary learning

10 Match the beginnings and endings of the sentences.

[h] Why don't you give
1 ☐ I tend to pick things
2 ☐ I can't get used
3 ☐ I'm getting
4 ☐ Do you want to have
5 ☐ She's making good
6 ☐ I got discouraged
7 ☐ I used to study for five hours every night but I couldn't keep
8 ☐ I'm finding it difficult but I'm going to persevere

- a a go?
- b when the teacher laughed at me.
- c progress.
- d better at it.
- e with it for a while.
- f up quite quickly.
- g it up.
- h ~~it a try?~~
- i to his accent.

test yourself!

Cover endings a to i above, and try to finish sentences 1 to 8 from memory.

how to
have a great conversation

natural English
asking follow-up questions

11 Rewrite the questions. Use the words given.

   A I work in customer relations.
   B What do you have to do?
     (involve) *What does that involve* ?
   A I mostly deal with customers who have questions or complaints.

1 A Just order them alphabetically.
   B Could you explain that a bit more clearly?
     (mean) _____?
   A Order them A, B, C, and so on.

2 A Sorry, but I can't come tonight.
   B Why?
     (How) _____?
   A I've got to work.

3 A I've just started a new course.
   B Really? How is it?
     (What) _____?
   A It's good – I'm enjoying it.

4 A Wear something nice tomorrow.
   B Like what?
     (sort) _____?
   A Something smart – a shirt and tie.

5 A I'm just going down to the shop.
   B Why?
     (for) _____?
   A We've run out of paper.

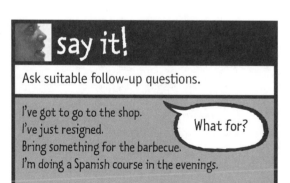

say it!

Ask suitable follow-up questions.

I've got to go to the shop.
I've just resigned.
Bring something for the barbecue.
I'm doing a Spanish course in the evenings.

What for?

---

expand
your vocabulary

learning and ability

Read the sentences below. Find underlined phrases that mean:

   to learn sth by chance rather than studying formally (1 phrase) _c_
1 to study hard in order to learn sth (1 phrase) ___
2 to have the ability to learn new things quickly and easily (3 phrases) ___ , ___ , ___
3 to be naturally very good at sth (usually an ability that you were born with) (4 phrases) ___ , ___ , ___ , ___

a He's got <u>a real flair for</u> design. I'm sure his fashion show will be absolutely spectacular.
b Don't ask me to do any maths! I really don't <u>have a head for</u> figures.
c ~~He picks up languages really easily. He spoke fluent French after living there for only a year.~~
d He missed the start of the course but he's <u>a fast learner</u>. In fact he's already as good as the others.
e She's only eight but she plays tennis brilliantly. She's <u>a natural</u>.
f She's very <u>quick on the uptake</u>. It didn't take her long at all to familiarize herself with our programme.
g I did well at college but it wasn't easy. I had to really <u>work at</u> it.
h He's a very <u>talented</u> young artist. He's already sold two of his paintings for a lot of money.
i I'm quite <u>quick at learning</u> things, but only if I'm genuinely interested in the subject.

> **We don't usually use the phrases in a, b, e, and h in the positive form to talk about ourselves, for example 'I have a flair for languages', because they sound immodest.**
> **Note some words that can follow these phrases.**
>   to have a flair for languages / art / writing
>   to be a talented musician / artist / actor
>   to have a head for figures / business

Cover the sentences above. Complete the sentences below with a suitable word.

  A He's really good at football!
  B Yes, he's a *natural*.
1 He has a _____ for languages.
2 I _____ things up really quickly.
3 I'm fairly quick _____ learning things if they interest me.
4 She's a _____ musician.
5 I don't have a _____ for figures.
6 I don't pick things up easily – I have to really _____ at it.
7 Can you explain that again? I'm not very quick on the _____!
8 She's quite a fast _____.

Tick the sentences that you might say about yourself, or that people might say about you.

two

start off

natural English *That was ... of you!*

1 Write responses. Use the words in the box.

clever	brave	kind	stupid	not / very nice	~~careless~~

The waitress knocked over my drink when she brought us the meal.   *That was careless of her*   .

1 He's afraid of heights but he went mountain-climbing anyway.   _____ .

2 I was going to call a taxi but my boss offered to give me a lift.   _____ .

3 I locked the keys in the car.   _____ .

4 She invited some of her colleagues to her party but none of them came.   _____ .

5 I solved your computer problem.   _____ .

 say it!

Cover the column on the right above and respond.

vocabulary physical actions

think back!

Look at the pictures. Remember the verbs for these physical actions.

2 Match the pictures and instructions.

Bend down and touch your toes.   *c*

1 Raise your hands above your head and reach up as if you were trying to touch the ceiling.   ___

2 Lean against the wall and raise your right leg. Hold it there for ten seconds.   ___

3 Now move away from the wall and keep your leg raised. If you lose your balance, just reach back and touch the wall again with your fingertips.   ___

4 Sit down, lean forward, and try to grab hold of your toes.   ___

5 Get down on your knees and stretch forward.   ___

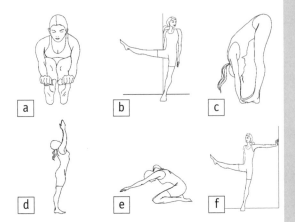

airport experiences

grammar *should* + infinitive

3 Write sentences with the same meaning. Use *should* or *shouldn't*.

There's a meeting for all new students in the main hall at 9.30 a.m.
All new students
should meet in the main hall at 9.30 a.m.

1 Passengers are not allowed to smoke anywhere inside the airport building.
Passengers _____ .

2 They left at 8.00, so I expect they'll be here by 10.00.
They left at 8.00, so they
_____ .

3 I don't think you'll have any trouble finding somewhere to stay.
You _____ .

4 I suggest that you talk to her as soon as possible and sort it out.
I think you _____ .

5 Add up the two numbers – I'm sure the total is 25.
Add up the two numbers – the total
_____ .

6 That address is wrong – it's Kenneth Road, not Tennis Road.
That address is wrong – it
_____ .

7 Don't wear that on the plane. You'll feel cold.
You _____ .

8 Start taking the tablets today and I think you'll feel better by tomorrow.
Start taking the tablets today and you
_____ .

grammar *should have* + past participle

4 What would you say about these situations? Complete the sentences. Use the verbs in brackets.

You went to an interview very casually dressed. The interviewer was very formal. You didn't get the job.
(wear) *I should've worn a suit* _____ .

1 You were only ten minutes late to meet some friends but they had already gone when you arrived.
(wait) They _____ .

2 Your friend left his car in front of a hospital. It was towed away.
(park) He _____ .

3 You had a huge lunch and now you feel sick.
(eat) I _____ .

4 You are stuck in traffic. You wish you hadn't driven.
(walk) We _____ .

5 Some bags were stolen from your friend's car.
(leave) She _____ .

say it!

Respond with your own ideas.

You are at a party, but you're not enjoying yourself because you've had a headache all day.

You turned down a job offer but now you wish you hadn't.

You've had a row with your girlfriend/boyfriend because you were late for a date.

Your friend didn't go to bed until 5.00 a.m. yesterday and now he's complaining that he's tired.

I should've taken something for my headache.

 **expand** your vocabulary

travel and holidays

Match these definitions to the words underlined in the quiz below.

	a new or difficult task that tests someone's ability or skill	_challenge_
1	a place you travel to	_____
2	relax	_____
3	very busy / chaotic	_____
4	write down the things you will need	_____
5	necessary things	_____
6	escape	_____
7	the excitement you feel when doing something thrilling or dangerous	_____
8	rest and get your energy back	_____
9	wanting to have a change	_____
10	schedule or plan	_____

Now do the quiz. Choose the answer that suits you best.

what kind of traveller are you?

The secret of having a great holiday is knowing what makes you happy.

I When, and what, do you normally pack for a holiday?
A *A week or two before, I choose coordinated, interchangeable clothes.*
B *The night before, I pack a couple of <u>essential items</u> in a backpack.*
C *I <u>make a checklist</u> a month or so ahead.*

2 Why do you usually take a holiday?
A *I have a <u>hectic</u> work schedule and need a break to <u>recharge</u>.*
B *I get <u>restless</u> or bored and just have to <u>get away</u> for some fun.*
C *I take a regular, allocated work break that best suits my employer.*

3 Which statement is most true for you?
A *I look at a couple of brochures and make a decision based on my interests and the cost.*
B *I want to go to a <u>destination</u> that offers the latest in sports or activities.*
C *I read a lot of brochures and make an <u>itinerary</u>, or I return to a place I've been before.*

4 What does a holiday mean to you?
A *It provides me with an opportunity to do many different things and have new experiences.*
B *I love a <u>challenge</u> and doing adventurous things.*
C *I gives me time to <u>wind down</u>.*

5 Which statement do you best relate to?
A *I like a mix of structured and less organized time.*
B *I want an <u>adrenalin rush</u> – whether on the dance floor or white-water rafting.*
C *I look for good food, a good pool, good tours, good service, and good value.*

Count up how many A, B, or C answers you have and read the conclusions below.

Mostly As **The intellectual traveller**
You need to combine learning with adventure, so go to a new place and explore the local culture. Book some short tours, or even a cookery or language course, but also allow time to relax. Don't go on a tour with a lot of people or return to the same destination each year.

Mostly Bs **The adventurous traveller**
You need a trip where you can have plenty of adrenalin rushes. You might enjoy learning a new sport, such as skiing or scuba diving. You would enjoy either travelling on your own or joining an adventure tour.

Mostly Cs **The organized traveller**
You'd enjoy a structured tour or a holiday with a group of friends. Choose a destination where the weather's great, the pool has a bar, and the gym offers massages.

test yourself!

Look at the first part again. Cover the words on the right. Read the definitions and try to remember the words.

tourist information

5 You're in a tourist information office. Complete the questions.

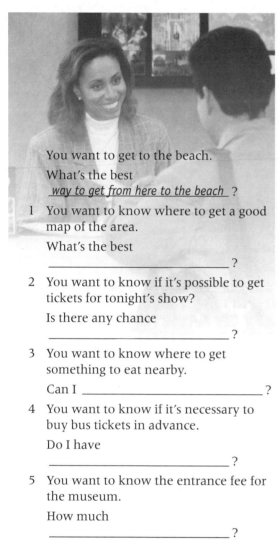

You want to get to the beach.

What's the best _way to get from here to the beach_ ?

1 You want to know where to get a good map of the area.

What's the best

_____ ?

2 You want to know if it's possible to get tickets for tonight's show?

Is there any chance

_____ ?

3 You want to know where to get something to eat nearby.

Can I _____ ?

4 You want to know if it's necessary to buy bus tickets in advance.

Do I have

_____ ?

5 You want to know the entrance fee for the museum.

How much

_____ ?

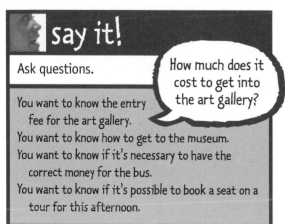

say it!

Ask questions.

How much does it cost to get into the art gallery?

You want to know the entry fee for the art gallery.

You want to know how to get to the museum.

You want to know if it's necessary to have the correct money for the bus.

You want to know if it's possible to book a seat on a tour for this afternoon.

grammar possibility and probability

6 Tick possible sentences. One, two, or three may be possible.

A Will Katia be at Peter's party?

B I shouldn't think so.
  a I doubt if she'll ✓
  b She's bound to
  c I dare say she'll
want to see Peter with his new girlfriend.

1
  a I don't suppose
  b It's likely that
  c I doubt if
we'll win. The other team's supposed to be brilliant.

2
  a I don't suppose they'll be late.
  b They're not likely to be late.
  c They'll probably be late.
Yeah, they always are!

3 Don't worry.
  a I doubt if everything will be OK.
  b Everything's bound to be OK.
  c I'm sure everything will be OK.

4
  a She might well
  b She'll definitely
  c She's highly likely to
need another operation. We won't know until tomorrow.

5
  a I probably won't get the job.
  b I shouldn't think I'll get the job.
  c I'm sure to get the job.
They are looking for someone with more experience.

6 She's studied so hard for these exams.
  a She's bound to pass.
  b I dare say she'll pass.
  c She'll definitely pass.

7
  a He's not likely to invite me
  b He might well invite me
  c I doubt if he'll invite me
to the wedding after the row I had with his girlfriend.

8 I'd love to have dinner there, but I can't afford it.
  a I shouldn't think it'll cost much.
  b It's sure to cost a fortune.
  c It probably won't cost too much.

7 Write sentences. Use the words given.

They / bound / be late.
They're bound to be late .

1 There / probably / not / be enough.
_____ .

2 I doubt / it / work.
_____ .

3 I dare say / Fabien / get the job.
_____ .

4 Things / unlikely / improve.
_____ .

5 I / not / suppose / they / lend me the money.
_____ .

6 The car / sure / break down.
_____ .

7 He / definitely / be there.
_____ .

8 Who / likely / win?
_____ ?

natural English *though* and *although*

8 Match the pairs of sentences.

g	Although the film had a lot of good actors in it,
1	I really like my job.
2	Although it was sunny,
3	Although I don't agree with him,
4	I only ate an hour ago.
5	Although it was a really cold day,
6	Although I haven't had anything to eat since breakfast,
7	The job itself is a bit boring.
8	I understand what he's saying.

a I'm not hungry at all.
b I meet a lot of interesting people, though.
c the water was warm enough to swim.
d I think he's got it all wrong, though.
e it was still quite cold.
f I'm quite hungry again, though.
g ~~it wasn't really very good.~~
h I can see his point of view.
i The pay's terrible, though.

expand your grammar

have sth done

We can use the structure *have* sth *done* (*have* + object + past participle) to talk about services that we ask or pay someone else to do for us.

I'm having my hair cut this afternoon.
(Someone else is going to cut it.)
I had the car fixed.
(Someone else fixed it and I paid them.)

Compare this to:

I fixed the car. (I fixed it myself.)

We can also use *get* instead of *have*.

Where did you get the car fixed?

We also use *have* sth *done* when things happen to us but we do not know who was responsible.

He had his wallet stolen.
(Someone stole his wallet.)

Complete the sentences below. Use the noun / verb pairs in the box, and *have* sth *done* in the correct tense. If the noun has already been used in the sentence, you must use a pronoun (as in the example).

~~hair / cut~~	phone / connect	jeans / take up
eyes / test	bag / steal	jacket / dry clean
house / paint	car / service	computer / fix

Your hair looks nice. Where _did you have it cut_ ?

1 If you can't read that sign, you should _____ .

2 I've bought some jeans but I need to _____ . They're much too long.

3 Can I get a lift to work with you? I _____ and I can't pick it up until tomorrow.

4 I can't tell you our number. We've just moved in and we _____ yet.

5 I'll have to _____ . I spilt some red wine on it.

6 My parents _____ at the moment so they're staying with me for a few days.

7 He _____ when he was walking home yesterday. A boy ran up to him and grabbed it.

8 Call me, as I can't check my e-mails. There's something wrong with my computer and I can't _____ until next week.

how to...
get the information you want

natural English asking for and making recommendations

9   Write sentences. Use the words given, in the correct form, and the information below.

Barcelona

PLACES OF INTEREST

Gaudi Cathedral - magnificent!

¹ Las Ramblas - avenue with cafes, bars and shops

² The Picasso Museum

DAY TRIPS

³ Sitges - beach resort

⁴ Figueres - where Salvador Dali used to live (his house is now a museum and art gallery)

⁵ The Miro Museum

    should / go / see
     You should go and see the Gaudi Cathedral. It's magnificent .

1 worth / take a walk along
    _____ .

2 recommend
    _____ .

3 worth / a visit
    _____ .

4 should / go / see
    _____ .

5 worth / go
    _____ .

write it!

You have received an e-mail from an English-speaking friend who is going to visit a city that you know. Write back to him, making some recommendations. Write about accommodation, places of interest, and things to see and do.

vocabulary tourists' phrases

think back!

Remember three types of accommodation you can stay in on holiday, and three things you can see or do on holiday.

10 Complete the text with suitable words.

ACCOMMODATION

If you want something cheap there are a lot of good camp _sites_ . You could also stay in youth ¹_____, which are quite basic, but OK. The other possibility is bed and ²_____ accommodation. If you just want to relax for a few days, there's a fantastic holiday ³_____ on the island.

SIGHTS

There are a lot of places of ⁴_____ in the city. I think it's worth going on a sightseeing ⁵_____ with a local guide. If you're really interested in historic ⁶_____ you should get your own guidebook. There are also some nice day ⁷_____ out of the city by bus or train. There's only one problem though - the admission ⁸_____ for the museums and galleries are really expensive.

three

start off

natural English *fancy (v)*

1 Rewrite the underlined sentences using *fancy*.

A Do you want to go to the cinema?
    Do you fancy going to the cinema ?

B Yeah, OK. What's on?

1 A Do you feel like something to eat?

_____?

B No, thanks. I only had lunch an hour ago.

2 A Let's go for a swim.

B I don't want to do that – the water will be freezing!

_____!

3 A You must be excited about moving into your new flat.

B Actually, I don't really like the idea of living there.

_____.

A Why not?

B It's not in a very nice area but it's all we can afford.

4 A Do you want a game of table tennis?

_____?

B Not now, but maybe later.

5 A We could go to Sparks for a drink.

B I'd like to go somewhere different.

_____.

say it!

Look at the pictures, and ask questions using *fancy*.

Do you fancy (getting) some food?

family ties

vocabulary
good and bad relationships

2 Complete the sentences. Use a verb from the box in the correct form.

communicate	hug	relate	consult
stick up for	~~quarrel~~	compete	get on	clash

The couple in the flat upstairs _quarrel_ all the time. I don't think they realize that we can hear them shouting.

1 My older brother and his friends always _____ with each other – especially about who's the best at sport or who's the most popular with the girls!

2 Pablo and Sonia are splitting up. She says that she can't _____ to him any more. Apparently he's changed a lot since he started this new job.

3 Don't you think that you should _____ a lawyer about this?

4 I _____ well with most of my colleagues. We see each other socially as well as at work.

5 My little brother gets embarrassed if Mum _____ him when she drops him off at school.

6 When we were at school together, Jonas used to _____ up for me when some of the other kids hit me.

7 I always _____ with my room-mate when I was at college. There was absolutely nothing we could agree on!

8 I like my boss but sometimes I find it quite difficult to _____ with him. He just won't listen to other people.

grammar *each other / one another, -self / -selves*

3 Choose the correct option.

   A How was your holiday?
   B Fantastic. I really enjoyed _myself_ .
     a me   b myself   c them   d (–)

1 A What did you do to your hand?
   B I cut _____ when I was slicing some bread.
     a me   b myself   c him   d (–)

2 My best friend and I talk to _____ on the phone every day.
     a us   b ourselves   c each other   d (–)

3 Can I help _____ with those bags? They look heavy.
     a me   b yourself   c you   d myself

4 Let's meet _____ at 6.00.
     a us   b ourselves   c me   d (–)

5 Let me introduce _____ . My name's Saori Matsuda.
     a me   b myself   c each other   d (–)

6 A You play the guitar really well.
   B My dad taught _____ how to play.
     a me   b yourself   c myself   d (–)

7 You need to concentrate _____ more if you're going to do well in class.
     a you   b yourself   c it   d (–)

8 We disagree with _____ about a lot of things.
     a ourselves   b us   c each other   d (–)

creating a community

grammar obligation, necessity, and prohibition

4 Carmen has just moved into a new flat. She has been given some information for tenants in the building. Read the text below.

Birley Lane apartments

REGULATIONS

A deposit is required before a **tenant** moves in.

1 Rent is payable two weeks in advance.
2 Tenants may not use the pool between 9.00 p.m. and 7.00 a.m.
3 No pets.
4 No smoking in common areas of the building.
5 Please be quiet when entering or leaving the building after 11.00 p.m.
6 The manager's permission is required for parties of more than ten people.
7 Do not hang pictures on the walls, paint the flat, or make other changes to the property without the owner's permission.
8 If something is broken or damaged, contact the manager. Do not repair it yourself.

The manager also tells Carmen about the regulations. Complete the sentences. Use the forms in the box below and a suitable verb.

mustn't	have to / have got to
don't have to	(not) be allowed (to)

You _'ve got to pay_____ a deposit before you move in.

1 You _____ rent two weeks in advance.

2 You _____ the pool between 9.00 p.m. and 7.00 a.m.

3 Pets _____ .

4 You _____ in your own flat but not in the common areas of the building.

5 You _____ quiet when you are coming home or going out after 11.00 p.m.

6 If you're having a small party (less than ten people), you _____ my permission.

7 You _____ pictures on the wall, paint the flat, or do anything like that without getting the owner's permission.

8 If you break or damage something, you _____ it yourself.

 **say it!**

Imagine that you and a friend have rented one of the apartments. Look at the information sheet above and tell your friend about the rules and regulations.

> We've got to pay a deposit before we move in.

expand your grammar

need

> *need* + **infinitive is slightly stronger in meaning than** *should* + **infinitive.**
>
> We need to do some shopping. The fridge is almost empty.
>
> I need to take a holiday – I'm exhausted.
>
> *need* + *-ing* **has a passive meaning. In this structure, the object of the verb comes at the beginning of the phrase.**
>
> Your shoes need cleaning.
>
> The car needs repairing.

Complete the conversations using the verbs given. Use either *need* + **infinitive or** *need* + *-ing*.

1 **A** Have you replied to Eva's e-mail?

   B No, not yet.

   A You _need to do_ (need/do) it as soon as possible – she wants to know what time we're arriving. Also, remember to phone the hotel this afternoon – we ¹ _____ (need/pay) the deposit before 5.00 p.m. today.

2 **A** I'm going shopping later. Do you need anything?

   B Yeah, some films for my camera and some sunblock.

   A I'll get those. By the way, the lock on the suitcase ² _____ (need/fix). Can you do it? And also my sunglasses ³ _____ (need/mend) – the little pin has come out.

3 **A** Can you get some cat food? We ⁴ _____ (need/leave) some here. You did ask Robert to come and feed her, didn't you?

   B Yes, but I think we ⁵ _____ (need/remind) him about it.

Write sentences about things you need to do, or which need doing, this week.

natural English agreeing with and challenging opinions

5 Maria is a teacher. She asks her students if they would like to change the way the classroom is organized. The classroom is currently like picture 1.

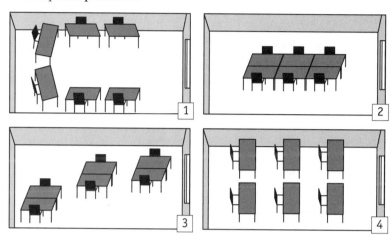

Complete the conversation. Use words from the box.

makes	right	~~why~~	say	seems	point

Maria I think we should move the tables around in here.

Jon I don't see _why_ . I like it the way it is.

Bianca I don't. It's claustrophobic.

Jon Why do you ¹ _____ that?

Bianca Well, you can't move around very easily.

James We could try putting all the desks together in the centre.

Bianca I don't see the ² _____ of that.

James Yes, but there'll be more space for all of us.

Maria Yes, that ³ _____ sense.

Elizabeth Wouldn't it be better to put the desks into three groups?

James Yes, I think you're ⁴ _____ .

Jon I'm still not sure.

Elizabeth Why don't we just try it for a week?

Maria Yes, that ⁵ _____ sensible. Does everyone agree?

Which classroom layout are they going to try?

say it!

Reply to these statements from other students, using the words given.

We should get more homework.	(see / why)
That was a boring class.	(why / say?)
I'm going to read more in English.	(see / point)
I'm only going to speak English at school.	(sensible)
I think we should use the dictionary for this exercise.	(sense)

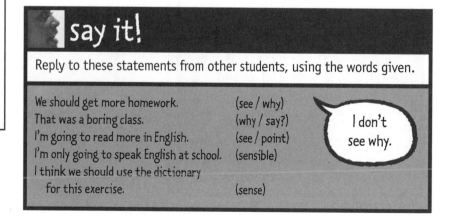

> I don't see why.

expand your vocabulary

personality

Match the adjectives and paraphrases.

	c	independent
1		thoughtless
2		outspoken
3		cheerful
4		outgoing
5		vivacious
6		vain
7		moody
8		laid-back
9		kind
10		chatty

a full of life

b concerned about his / her appearance

c ~~doesn't rely on other people~~

d happy one minute and unhappy the next

e usually very relaxed

f often speaks or acts without thinking of others

g likes to speak his / her mind

h confident and sociable

i always has a smile on his / her face

j has a heart of gold

k loves to talk

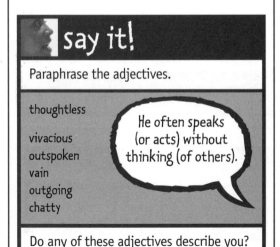

say it!

Paraphrase the adjectives.

thoughtless

vivacious

outspoken

vain

outgoing

chatty

He often speaks (or acts) without thinking (of others).

Do any of these adjectives describe you?

wordbooster

personality phrases

think back!

Remember five words to describe someone's personality.

6 Put these sentences into the magazine article below.

a I'm sure that Mum and Dad think that I'm totally <u>out of control</u>

b I don't try to hide the fact that I want to <u>get on in life</u>.

c I'm sure my staff think that I can be <u>a pain in the neck</u>.

d I think my friends would say that I'm <u>a good laugh</u>.

e ~~I'm sure some people might think I've got a big ego.~~

How others see you, *how you see yourself*

How do you think family, friends, or colleagues would describe your personality? Do you think they're right?

CLARA, *21, student*

1 *e* but in fact I'm quite shy. Because I'm really not very self-confident I try to come across as outgoing and self-assured.

CARLOS, *18, student*

2 ___ but I don't think I am. I like to think of myself as a bit wild! I just like to try everything once and live life to the full.

MARTIN, *26, banker*

3 ___ Some people probably think that I'm a bit too ambitious and obsessed with work, but I won't be happy unless I get to the top!

FELIX, *22, unemployed*

4 ___ I do like to be funny but I sometimes think that people don't see that I've got a serious and sensitive side too.

PAOLA, *38, manager*

5 ___ I'm very fussy about what time people get to work, how they dress, and the standard of their work, but that's my job!

how to...
write a website profile

natural English linking ideas

7 Combine the sentences. Use a non-finite clause.

The man was completely lost. He stopped a passerby and asked for directions.
Completely lost, the man stopped a passerby and asked for directions .

1 The company was set up ten years ago in Holland. It is now one of the world's leading software makers.

_____ .

2 Gabriella is a very experienced teacher. She is excited about taking on the position of headmistress.

_____ .

3 Dae-Sang is the son of an architect. He has always been interested in design.

_____ .

4 The company is expanding rapidly. It now needs bigger premises.

_____ .

5 Jackie is currently studying languages. She would like to work as a translator when she finishes college.

_____ .

grammar sequencing information in a text

8 Combine the sentences. Use the words given.

He left school. He soon found a job he liked.
(shortly after) Shortly _after leaving school he found a job he liked_ .

1 It was almost dawn. My alarm clock went off.
(shortly before) My _____ .

2 Before you have the interview, you should find out as much as you can about the company.
(prior to) Prior _____ .

3 We were friends. He became famous later.
(long before) We _____ .

4 They met. A short time later they got engaged.
(soon after) They _____ .

5 I gave up smoking. I feel a lot better now.
(since) I feel _____ .

write it!

Use the notes about Leonardo DiCaprio to write a website biography of the actor.

LEO – The early years

Born Hollywood November 11th 1974

Mother (German immigrant) & father (artist) separated shortly after his birth

Parents encouraged acting

Aged 2 – TV-show Romper Room

Elementary school – acting classes

High school – plays, advertisements, educational films and TV shows

1991 first film – horror film Critters 3

1993 film This Boy's Life – **career breakthrough**

1993 film What's Eating Gilbert Grape? (with Johnny Depp) – won Oscar nomination for best supporting actor

1996 played Romeo in Romeo and Juliet – became an international star

glossary
career breakthrough /kəˈrɪə ˈbreɪkθruː/ the film that first brought him attention

four

Tick (✓) when you've done these sections.

natural English
- ☐ frequency phrases
- ☐ 'sitting on the fence'
- ☐ making and responding to requests

grammar
- ☐ nouns in groups
- ☐ future simple and continuous
- ☐ expand your grammar future perfect

vocabulary
- ☐ adjectives describing reactions
- ☐ the language of editing
- ☐ words of similar meaning
- ☐ expand your vocabulary phrases with *of*

start off

vocabulary adjectives describing reactions

think back!

Remember other adjectives that have similar meanings to *surprising*, *annoying*, and *peculiar*.

1 Underline the adjective that best describes each situation.

You are walking home from work one evening. It starts to rain hard. You decide to get a taxi but none come for ten minutes. Then three go past but don't stop for you.

<u>annoying</u> / odd / astonishing

1 You hadn't studied hard at all, so you were dreading getting your exam results. When they came, though, they were really good.

surprising / peculiar / annoying

2 A man approaches you in the street and acts as if you are old friends. He asks you about your family and if they are OK. You explain that he has confused you with someone else but he seems surprised that you don't know him.

astonishing / infuriating / strange

3 Your neighbours are having a party and are being really noisy. You went to bed at 11.30 p.m. It's now 1.00 a.m. and you're still not asleep.

weird / amazing / irritating

don't believe everything you see in films

natural English frequency phrases

2 Match the beginnings and endings of the phrases.

How often do you go to the cinema?

e	Quite
1	About twice a
2	Whenever
3	Hardly
4	Every month
5	Once in
6	Roughly once
7	It
8	Now and

a I can.
b or so.
c again.
d a fortnight.
e ~~often~~.
f varies.
g week.
h a while.
i ever.

grammar nouns in groups

3 Complete the sentences using the words in brackets. Add any other necessary words or punctuation.

I took this photo from the _top of the mountain_ (mountain / top). The view's spectacular, isn't it?

1 I'm usually exhausted by _____ (day / end).
2 My _____ (player / DVD) was stolen from my car.
3 Have you seen _____ (paper / today)?
4 My sister is a _____ (artist / make-up). She usually works with models on photo shoots but occasionally she does some work on films.
5 My _____ (boss / husband) has asked him to work late every night this week.
6 Have you got a _____ (opener / bottle) I can use?
7 Try to get a good _____ (sleep / night). You'll feel better in the morning.
8 Oh, no! I can't find my _____ (keys / house). I hope I haven't locked them inside!

say it!

Answer the questions using frequency phrases.

How often do you ... ?
... go to the cinema?
... buy magazines?
... go out with friends?
... speak English (outside class)?
... use the Internet?

About once a month.

say it!

Describe these places using *end / bottom / corner / beginning*.

the bottom of the sea

the mobile phone police

natural English 'sitting on the fence'

4 Complete the sentences with a suitable word.

> **Q** **Should children be allowed to own mobile phones?**
>
> I can see both _sides_ . I don't really think kids need a mobile. On the other hand, it makes kids and parents feel safer if they know they can call home whenever they need to.
>
> 1 It's a difficult _____ . I do think that they're useful for kids to have, but we don't know the long-term health effects of using them.
>
> 2 It _____ , doesn't it? If they're just calling a friend for a chat they don't need a mobile, but if they're going out somewhere then they're useful.
>
> 3 It's hard to _____ . I've had a mobile since I was 13 but I've never used it that much. To be honest, I could live without it.

grammar future simple and continuous

5 Underline the correct form.

What do you think you'll do / <u>'ll be doing</u> this time next year?

1 Give it to me and I'll give / 'll be giving it to Sam. I'm seeing her later.

2 We'll play / 'll be playing football all afternoon, so if you want to join us just come along to the park.

3 I won't call / won't be calling you until I get some more news.

4 By the end of the month we'll have / 'll be having enough money to buy a car.

5 Do you think you'll still work / 'll still be working here next year?

6 Maybe we shouldn't go round at the weekend. They'll pack / 'll be packing everything up to move.

7 Don't ring the boss this afternoon. He'll do / 'll be doing interviews until 5.00 p.m.

8 Don't worry. I won't forget / won't be forgetting to tell him.

6 Sophie and Julia work for the same company but in different cities. Complete their e-mails below. Use the verbs in brackets in either the future simple or future continuous.

---

from: Julia   **subject:** holiday

Hi Sophie

I just wanted to let you know that I' _ll be_ (be) on holiday for the next two weeks (this time next week I ¹ _____ (lie) on the beach!). My colleague Jason ² _____ (do) my job while I'm away so I ³ _____ (give) him all of the information. Call him if you need to know anything.

Cheers, Julia

---

from: Sophie   **subject:** RE: holiday

Dear Julia

I hope you have a good holiday! It's a pity that you ⁴ _____ (not / be) there next week, as I'm hoping to visit in person. I ⁵ _____ (leave) the stuff you asked for with Jason. I think that by the end of the month we ⁶ _____ (have) enough information to complete the report, don't you? Otherwise we ⁷ _____ (still / work) on it over Christmas, which would be a nightmare!

Think of me stuck in the office while you're on the beach! ⁸ _____ (you / get) in touch as soon as you get back?

Sophie

expand your grammar

future perfect

We use the future perfect (*will* (*not*) + *have* + past participle) to refer to an action that will happen or will be finished before a point of time in the future.

By the time we see her again, Jane will have started her new job.

now _____X_____X_____ future
                  start new job   see her again

By the time I'm 40, I'll have bought a house.

now _____X_____X_____ future
                buy house   40th birthday

Complete the sentences. Use the verbs in brackets in the future perfect.

Let's set off after 10.00 a.m. The rush hour *will have finished* (finish) by then.

1 Hurry up! If we don't leave right now, the film (start) _____ by the time we get there.

2 _____ (they / make) a decision by the end of today?

3 At the end of this month my parents (be) _____ married for fifty years.

4 Hopefully, by the time I see you again, I _____ (find) a job.

5 I'll call you around 8.00. You _____ (not /go) out by then, will you?

Complete the sentences. Use the verbs in brackets in the correct form (future simple, future continuous, or future perfect).

What will your life be like in ten years' time?

Robert, *23, student*
I don't think my life *will be* _____ (be) all that different to now. I expect I *'ll be living* _____ (live) in the same place but, with any luck, I *'ll have found* _____ (find) a job that I enjoy.

Jorge, *22, teacher*
Hopefully, by then I [1] _____ (meet) the woman of my dreams and we [2] _____ (live) in luxury somewhere sunny.

Miroslav, *35, accountant*
I hope I [3] _____ (retire) by then, having earned an absolute fortune!

Yuki, *25, advertising executive*
I [4] _____ (probably / do) the same kind of work as I am now, only hopefully I [5] _____ (earn) a lot more money! Who knows – maybe I [6] _____ (buy) the company!

Susie, *20, secretary*
I expect I [7] _____ (still / live) in London and I hope [8] _____ (be) married. I [9] _____ (probably / have) a couple of children.

Martin, *18, medical student*
It's hard to say, but I guess I [10] _____ (work) in a hospital or family medical practice.

say it!

What do you think your life will be like in 10 years' time? What about in 20?

expand your vocabulary

phrases with *of*

Look at these words and definitions.

means of	a way of achieving or doing sth
	a means of transport = a way of getting around
rate of	the measurement of the amount, or speed, of change over a period of time
	the rate of inflation (or inflation rate) = the amount and speed by which prices in a country are rising
sense of	a feeling about sth
	a sense of achievement = the positive feeling you get when you have achieved something
standard of	the quality of
	the standard of living = the quality of life people have
level of	the amount of sth at a particular time
	the level of alcohol in sb's blood = how much alcohol someone has in their blood at a particular time

Match the words in the box with the phrases below.

unemployment	communication	~~pollution~~	direction	education

	level of	*pollution*
1	rate of	_____
2	sense of	_____
3	standard of	_____
4	means of	_____

Complete the sentences with a suitable phrase from above.

The _rate of unemployment_ went up by 10% last year.

1 Government ministers are meeting conservation groups and scientists to discuss how the _____ in our rivers can be reduced.

2 The _____ has gone up by 3% so far this year and prices are still rising.

3 Even though he didn't come first, he got a real _____ from doing well.

4 The _____ in our primary schools is deteriorating. The government needs to spend more on this area.

5 The bike is by far the most popular _____ in Vietnam.

6 Our _____ is fairly high compared to other countries, but there is still a big difference between the rich and the poor.

7 Don't ask me which way to go – I've got a terrible _____ .

8 E-mail is now the most widely used _____ .

wordbooster

words of similar meaning

7 Complete the text. Use the verbs in the box in the correct form.

control	improve	~~grow~~	prohibit
deteriorate	limit	cut	examine	increase

Memo

Date 18/12/02
To all staff
From the Managing Director

A big thank you to all of our staff. It has been an excellent year and the company _has grown_ considerably. Sales went up by 30% and next year we intend to
1 _____ the number of staff from 455 to 510.

Last year the amount spent on entertaining clients was excessive, so next year we have to
2 _____ expenditure on corporate entertainment by 25%.

We are going to introduce a new system for 3 _____ the quality of goods. From now on, all goods must be 4 _____ three times, twice by machine and once by hand, before being packaged. We hope that this
5 _____ the number of faulty goods.

We are committed to 6 _____ working conditions for all employees. We realize that the standard of all of the office equipment 7 _____ a lot recently and we appreciate your tolerance. The offices will be refurbished in April 2003.

We are planning to 8 _____ smoking in all parts of the building from January 2003 onwards. Smokers, please use the rooftop terrace.

test yourself!

Look again at the verbs in the box above. For each one, try to remember another verb with a similar meaning.

how to... write and edit e-mails

natural English making and responding to requests

8 Write requests. Use the words given.

lend me some money
(wondering) *I was wondering if you could lend me some money?*

1 post this letter for me
(think) _____ ?

2 have a look at my computer
(chance) _____ ?

3 proofread this report that I've written
(wondering) _____ ?

4 get some bread on your way home
(think) _____ ?

5 give me a lift to the station
(chance) _____ ?

Match these responses to the requests.

a Leave it on my desk and I'll see what I can do. _____

b Sure. I'm going past the post office later anyway. _____

c I've only got a couple of dollars myself. _example_

d Sure. What time? _____

e I don't know that much about them. _____

f Yes, but I won't be home until late. _____

vocabulary the language of editing

9 Read the essay and complete the teacher's notes below.

> ARE LETTERS OR E-MAILS THE BEST MEANS OF COMMUNICATION?
>
> There is no doubt that e-mail has enabled us to com^municate with each other much more quickly than in the past but is e-mail unquestionably a good thing¹? Letters tend to take us longer to write, but perhaps we think more about what we are saying. In e-mails we don't worry so much about correct spelling or punctuation.² ~~If~~ we make a mistake, we can just call it a typo. We also keep letters for longer, so if we can't remember what a friend said in their last letter we can just look at it again. However, we usually ³WT deleted our e-mails. ⁴NP! On the other hand,⁵ when we need a quick response, e-mail is perfect.⁶ ~~Its~~ It's also cheap, and much more convenient than sending a letter because we don't need to leave our desk⁷(and we don't have to queue in the post-⁸office!)

You need a _double m_ !

1 Don't forget to put a _____ . You are asking a question.

2 These are two separate sentences so you need a _____ and a capital letter.

3 Wrong _____ . It should be present simple.

4 Start a new _____ here.

5 'On the other hand' should be followed by a _____ .

6 Remember – when you mean 'It is' you need an _____ .

7 You could put this in _____ , or leave it out, as it's not so important.

8 'Post office' doesn't need a _____ .

five

Tick (✓) when you've done these sections.

natural English
- [ ] talking about test / exam results
- [ ] expectation and surprise
- [ ] spoken v. written English
- [ ] *not that* + adjective

grammar
- [ ] narrative tenses
- [ ] modifying and intensifying adverbs
- [ ] expand your grammar
      modifiers + *too* + adjective

vocabulary
- [ ] taking exams
- [ ] phrasal verbs
- [ ] *so* and *such*
- [ ] expand your vocabulary
      formal and informal verbs

start off

natural English talking about test / exam results

1 Here are the test results for some students in an English class. Match the names of the students to the sentences below. Sometimes more than one answer is possible.

Name	Final result	Grade	Pass / fail (pass = 50%)
Young-Eun	70%	B	P
Ralph	93%	A	P
Alberto	15%	E	F
Nina	52%	C	P
Tomoko	47%	D	F

I got an A.		*Ralph*
1	I did well.	_____
2	I only just failed.	_____
3	I got excellent marks.	_____
4	I just passed.	_____
5	I did very badly.	_____

 say it!

Look at the results table again and talk about the results.

> Ralph got an A.

what an experience!

grammar narrative tenses

2 Underline the correct form.

Why <u>didn't you tell</u> / weren't you telling me that you'd already got a ticket?

1 When I arrived they had already started / had already been starting lunch.

2 A What did you do / were you doing there?

  B Waiting for my sister to pick me up.

3 We drove / were driving along the motorway when we got a flat tyre.

4 We hadn't waited / hadn't been waiting for long but it was raining and we were getting cold so we left.

5 I didn't want to go because I'd seen / 'd been seeing the film before.

6 I just thought / was just thinking about you when you rang.

7 I found out later that they'd made / 'd been making a mistake.

8 They 'd gone out / 'd been going out together for ages so it came as a big surprise to us when they broke up.

3 Complete the newspaper article. Use the verbs in brackets in the correct form (past simple, past continuous, past perfect simple, or past perfect continuous).

Two determined women went **bonnet**-to-bonnet for one parking space, a court was told yesterday.

Last December Julie Brown, 43, <u>drove</u> (drive) into the space in the middle of the High Street, only to be confronted by Melanie Andrews, 20, coming from the opposite direction. Both women ¹ _____ (believe) they ² _____ (see) the space first and both ³ _____ (refuse) to move. In a grinding of metal and smoke, Ms Andrews then ⁴ _____ (**shunt**) her rival out of the space, despite the fact that Mrs Brown ⁵ _____ (apply) her handbrake and her twelve-year-old son Dominic ⁶ _____ (stand) behind her car, pushing back. Later Ms Andrews claimed that she ⁷ _____ (wait) for the previous car to vacate the spot and that consequently the spot was rightfully hers.

A jury at Winchester Crown Court ⁸ _____ (find) Andrews guilty of dangerous driving. Liz Gunther, for the prosecution, said: 'Parking **rage** is the best way to describe this case.'

glossary

bonnet /ˈbɒnɪt/ the metal part over the front of a car, usually covering the engine

shunt /ʃʌnt/ to push sth violently

rage /reɪdʒ/ a feeling of violent anger

natural English
expectation and surprise

4 Tick the correct options. One, two, or three may be correct.

I thought that the job interview had been terrible, but to my surprise

a they offered me the job. ✓

b I didn't get the job. ✗

c they've asked me to go back for a second interview. ✓

1 I didn't do any revision for the test, but to my amazement

a I passed.

b I failed.

c I did very badly.

2 He was an hour late to meet his girlfriend, so when he arrived, as you might expect,

a she had gone home.

b she was furious.

c they had an argument.

3 She was late for work for the third time in a week, so inevitably

a her boss didn't mind.

b no one seemed to care.

c her boss was annoyed with her.

4 Ricky was at the party, but

a he went home early.

b he didn't stay for long.

c he ignored me.

5 My brother doesn't usually remember my birthday, but this year to my surprise

a he forgot.

b he gave me a present.

c he sent me a card.

wordbooster

taking exams

EXAM IN PROGRESS SILENCE PLEASE!

think back!

Remember five verbs connected with exams.

5 Some students are discussing an exam they've just taken. Complete the sentences with verbs / phrases from the box, in the correct form.

get through	make a mess	retake	turn up	cheat	sit	fail
take place	(not) come up	~~prepare~~	bluff my way through			

If I _had prepared_ for the test, I'm sure I could've got good marks in it.

1 I _____ a minute late and the invigilator wouldn't let me in.

2 I'm sure I _____ . I wasn't sure about any of the answers.

3 If I don't pass, I'll _____ the exam next month.

4 Where's the speaking test going to _____ ?

5 I _____ of the listening test! I got it all wrong.

6 I was surprised that phrasal verbs _____ in the test yesterday.

7 If I _____ that part of the exam, then I think I'll pass the rest.

8 Jacob's been disqualified for _____ . Apparently, he was trying to copy from the student next to him.

9 I've got to _____ another test this afternoon.

10 Although I didn't know much about it, I think I managed to _____ the essay question.

phrasal verbs

6 Complete the sentences. Use phrasal verbs with *go*, *turn*, *get* and *come*, in the correct form. The meaning of the missing phrasal verb is given in brackets.

Isn't your birthday _coming up_ soon?
(happen)

1 I like this song. Could you _____ it _____ ?
(increase the volume)

2 I tried to call you this afternoon but I couldn't _____ .
(be connected)

3 There's a lot of noise in the background. What's _____ ?
(happen)

4 What time did they eventually _____ ?
(arrive)

5 His leg has been badly injured, but as time _____ he'll find it easier to move around.
(pass)

6 She got such a fright. She didn't realize he was there, and he _____ behind her and tapped her on the shoulder.
(approach)

7 I thought I'd lost my credit card but it _____ at my parents' house.
(appear)

8 I'll have to study late tonight – I've got so much work to _____ for my exams.
(finish)

write it!

Write about a time when you took an exam.

 **a test** of endurance

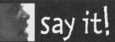 **say it!**

Say sentences about these things using an adjective and modifier or intensifier.

The last film you saw.
The last test you took.
A book you read recently.
Today's weather.

I watched a movie on TV last night. It was absolutely awful.

grammar modifying and intensifying adverbs

7 Complete the sentences. Use a suitable extreme adjective.

    A   It's extremely hot in here, isn't it?

    B   Yes, it's _boiling_ !

1 A   I'm quite tired. I think I'll go home now.

    B   Yes, me too. I'm _____ !

2 A   It was really frightening wasn't it?

    B   _____ ! I hate films like that. I probably won't be able to sleep tonight.

3 A   Did you have a good time?

    B   Yes, _____ !

4 A   I've read this book too.

    B   What did you think of it?

    A   To be honest, I thought it was pretty bad.

    B   Me too. I thought it was absolutely _____ !

5 A   It's a stupid idea, isn't it?

    B   I think it's the most _____ thing I've ever heard!

8 Underline the correct words. One, two, or three may be possible.

The film was rather / <u>really</u> / <u>absolutely</u> fantastic.

1 I thought that it would be difficult but in fact it was really / fairly / absolutely easy.

2 A   Did you enjoy the film?

    B   No! The story was extremely / really / absolutely ridiculous.

3 His job is pretty / rather / extremely stressful, isn't it?

4 A   What's the weather like there today?

    B   Pretty / Really / Absolutely nice!

5 It was a fairly / rather / absolutely unpleasant journey as our air-conditioning wasn't working.

6 The food was good but the service was fairly / extremely / absolutely appalling.

7 A   How's your course going?

    B   I'm enjoying it, but it's rather / fairly / really challenging.

8 A   Was the test difficult?

    B   Rather / Fairly / Absolutely impossible!

natural English
spoken v. written English

9 Replace the underlined words with less formal words from the box, in the correct form. Keep the meaning the same.

~~find out~~	cut off	get rid of
take part in	take up	turn out
work out	come to an end	tell off

In our research we are trying to <u>discover</u> how sleep can be affected by different foods. _find out_

1 If we don't pay the bill this week, the phone will be <u>disconnected</u>.

    _____

2 I think the government <u>abolished</u> that law two years ago. _____

3 I was often <u>reprimanded</u> by the teachers at school. _____

4 If you want to <u>participate in</u> any of the water sports at the club you have to sign this insurance document first.

    _____

5 As it <u>transpired</u>, I had a room to myself.

    _____

6 Studying <u>occupies</u> most of my time.

    _____

7 When the course <u>terminated</u> we didn't see each other for five years.

    _____

8 Once I can <u>determine</u> where the fault is, I'll be able to fix it for you.

    _____

expand your vocabulary

formal and informal verbs

Verbs 1 to10 below are more formal than verbs a to k. You might use the more formal ones when writing, or when speaking to someone you don't know, often in a work situation. You might use the less formal ones when speaking to people you know.

Match verbs with the same meaning.

	purchase	*i*	a	let sb know
1	cancel		b	say sorry
2	request		c	put off
3	obtain		d	get
4	ascertain		e	call off
5	inform		f	get in touch with sb
6	apologize		g	ask for
7	require		h	sort out
8	contact		i	~~buy~~
9	postpone		j	need
10	resolve		k	find out

Cover the exercise above. Make the underlined verbs below less formal.

Where did you <u>purchase</u> it?
 buy

1 If you <u>require</u> any more information, please call me. _____

2 I'm trying to <u>ascertain</u> exactly why she's resigned. _____

3 I <u>requested</u> a room with a view but they didn't have any. _____

4 I think you should <u>apologize</u> to her.
 _____

5 They have <u>postponed</u> the wedding until later in the year. _____

6 I am calling to <u>inform you</u> that I won't be able to meet you on Friday.
 _____

7 Why was the match <u>cancelled</u>?
 _____

8 Have you <u>resolved</u> the problem with your computer yet? _____

9 I'm trying to <u>contact</u> Simona Gentile. You don't know her number, do you?
 _____

10 You can <u>obtain</u> copies of the document from our head office. _____

how to... emphasize what you feel

vocabulary *so* and *such*

10 Write sentences with the same meaning. Use *so* or *such*.

It's such a new design that not many people have seen it yet.
The design is <u>*so new that not many people have seen it yet.*</u> .

1 The film was so boring that we walked out halfway through.
 It _____ .

2 We had such bad weather that we decided to come home early.
 The weather _____ .

3 It was such a difficult test that I gave up.
 The test _____ .

4 The food was so disgusting that I didn't eat a thing!
 It _____ .

5 His results were so good that he decided to go to college after all.
 He _____ .

6 It was such a loud noise that I closed the window.
 The noise _____ .

7 The teacher's so good that I've decided to attend his class again next term.
 He _____ .

8 It's such an old car that I'm not at all surprised it broke down.
 The car _____ .

natural English *not that* + adjective

11 Match the pairs of sentences.

	f	You didn't miss much.
1		The test wasn't that difficult.
2		Let's think it through again.
3		You can't be that hungry.
4		Stop worrying about your interview.
5		I didn't think the film was that bad.

a We had dinner only an hour ago.
b I'm sure it won't be that bad.
c It can't be that complicated.
d It could've been much harder.
e Catherine Zeta Jones was good, didn't you think?
f ~~The party really wasn't that good.~~

expand your grammar

modifiers + *too* + adjective

Look at these examples.

too + adjective

   A Do you want to go swimming?

   B No, it's too cold!

too + adjective + for + sb

   These jeans are too small for me.

too + adjective + infinitive

   I feel too sick to go to school.

We often use modifiers before *too*.

Far, miles, and *way* all mean the same as *much* (but *miles* and *way* are more informal).

   That jacket looks much too big.

   I'm far too hungry to wait any longer.

   It's miles too big for you.

   It's way too hot to play tennis today.

Slightly and *a bit* mean the same as *a little* (but *a bit* is more informal).

   The dessert's a little too sweet for me.

   The sofa's slightly too big to get through the door.

   It's a bit too far to walk there.

Complete the sentences. Use the words given.

   They had to stop the match. It be / bit / dark / see the ball.

   It was a bit too dark to see the ball.

1 By the time I finally finished work it be / much / late / go / cinema.

   _____

2 It's a nice shirt but that size look / little / small / you.

   _____

3 I need something to eat now. I be / way / hungry / wait / dinner.

   _____

4 We should get the bus. It take / far / long / walk there.

   _____

5 I'm not coming to the party. I be / bit / tired.

   _____

6 There's no point in us talking about it now. I can see that you be / way / angry / listen to me.

   _____

7 I'm going to have to cut out some of this essay. It be / slightly/ long.

   _____

8 Do you want this jacket? It be / miles / big / me.

   _____

say it!

Respond to the questions using the words given and a modifier of your choice.

Did you read the book in English?
No / difficult / me.

> No, it was way too difficult for me!

Do you want to come to the beach?
No / cold / me.

Do you want a lift home?
No / early / leave.

Shall we watch a video?
No / late / start watching a film.

six

Tick (✓) when you've done these sections.

natural English
- [ ] talking about needs
- [ ] *apparently, it appears / seems that*
- [ ] getting sb's attention

grammar
- [ ] past simple and present perfect passive
- [ ] indirect questions
- [ ] expand your grammar other passive forms

vocabulary
- [ ] feelings and emotions
- [ ] collocation
- [ ] expressing opinions and interest
- [ ] dangers and disasters
- [ ] knowing your prepositions
- [ ] expand your vocabulary phrases with *in* and *on*

start off

vocabulary feelings and emotions

think back!

Remember three phrases to describe how you feel after getting good news and three after getting bad news.

1 Match sentences 1 to 5 to the responses a to f.

So we've set a date for the wedding – it's going to be September 2nd. _e_

1 Do you remember that job I had an interview for last month? Well, I got it! I start next week. ___

2 Did you know that Juan and Paulina have broken up? Apparently she's met another man. ___

3 My sister's got into the national swimming team. She's hoping to go to the next Olympic Games. ___

4 She promised that we would do the project together. Then she decided to do it with Jane instead. ___

5 He had been doing all this overtime and working really late. Then they offered the promotion to someone else. ___

a You must have felt really let down.

b Oh no! He must be heartbroken.

c Oh! I expect he's really fed up.

d Wow! You must be thrilled to bits.

e ~~Your mum and dad must be over the moon. They love Alessandro, don't they?~~

f Really? She must be ecstatic.

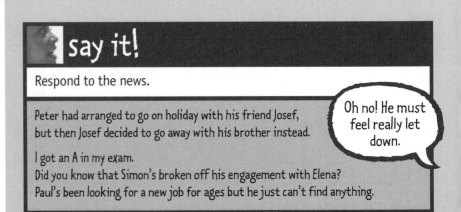

say it!

Respond to the news.

Peter had arranged to go on holiday with his friend Josef, but then Josef decided to go away with his brother instead.

I got an A in my exam.
Did you know that Simon's broken off his engagement with Elena?
Paul's been looking for a new job for ages but he just can't find anything.

Oh no! He must feel really let down.

trouble spots

natural English talking about needs

2 Could you survive on a desert island for three months with only nine other people?

What would you need to survive? Match the pairs of sentences.

<u>I couldn't live without</u> my friends! `[e]`

1 Music <u>would be absolutely essential</u>. `[ ]`

2 <u>I'd have to have</u> some privacy! `[ ]`

3 <u>I'd have to take</u> a supply of cigarettes with me. `[ ]`

4 <u>I couldn't survive without</u> chocolate! `[ ]`

5 Some good books <u>would be essential.</u> `[ ]`

a If I could have my own tent then it might be OK, but I'd hate to share with anyone.

b I'd worry about it melting though!

c Especially as it doesn't sound as if there's much else to do there!

d I'd have to have a mini-disc player to keep my sanity.

e ~~Being alone with nine strangers would drive me crazy.~~

f I'm afraid I get through a packet a day.

say it!

Say what you would take with you to a desert island. Use the underlined phrases in exercise 2, and the pictures below, to help you.

I'd have to have some coffee with me!

vocabulary collocation

think back!

Look at these news headlines. Think of three words that you might expect to find in each story.

> **Earthquake destroys city**
>
> **Rebels attack national TV station**
>
> **Police hunt for girl's attacker**

3 Complete the news stories with words from the box.

terrorist	latest	extremely	control
vitally	surrounding	under	seriously
~~completely~~	fire	badly	

Earthquake destroys city

PARTS OF THE CITY have been _completely_ destroyed. Buildings in ¹ _____ areas have also been ² _____ damaged. The ³ _____ information we have received suggests that over 500 people have been killed and up to 2,000 ⁴ _____ injured. Fires in the north of the city are now burning out of ⁵ _____ .

Rebels attack national TV station

REBELS HAVE ATTACKED the national TV station. Government forces soon had the situation ⁶ _____ control, but not before rebels had set fire to part of the studio building, which is still on ⁷ _____ now. Fighting between rebel and government forces has escalated in recent weeks and this is the third ⁸ _____ attack in the capital this month.

Police hunt for girl's attacker

POLICE HAVE ASKED FOR anyone who recognizes this man to come forward. The man is wanted in connection with an assault on a teenage girl on Monday. Any information is ⁹ _____ important, however trivial it may seem. They say that the man is ¹⁰ _____ dangerous and that under no circumstances should he be approached.

wordbooster

dangers and disasters

4 Complete the sentences with nouns formed from the verbs in the box.

warn	~~explode~~	kidnap	arrest	survive
injure	accuse	threaten	evacuate	

The _explosion_ destroyed the shopping centre.

1 Police say that they were given no _____ of the bomb so they were unable to evacuate the area.

2 The _____ of the three men lost on the mountain will depend on the weather over the next two days.

3 Police have made several _____ following violent demonstrations outside the government building.

4 Racing driver Stan Portman has crashed in the Monaco Grand Prix. Doctors say that his _____ are serious, although he is in a stable condition.

5 The _____ have come as a complete surprise to the ambassador, who denies any involvement in the case.

6 This is the third _____ of a politician's family member in six months, and the financial demands are always the same.

7 Police say that there is no immediate _____ to villages to the south of the volcano.

8 The _____ started three hours ago. People are leaving the towns with as much as they can pack into their cars or carry on their backs.

write it!

Look at the headline and write a short news story. Use the words given to help you.

> shopping centre / 50 people / shops and cars
>
> explode / injure / damage / warn / evacuate
>
> **Bomb damages city centre.**

knowing your prepositions

5 Underline the correct preposition.

One thousand people were evacuated at / <u>from</u> / in the area.

1 The man accused me in / on / of stealing his wallet.

2 The police arrested him of / for / from drink-driving.

3 Airport staff are searching people at / in / on random.

4 The charity is on / in / of need of more donations.

5 You should wear sunblock to protect your skin at / of / from the sun.

have you heard?

grammar past simple and present perfect passive

6 Underline the correct form.

    A That's a nice picture.

    B It painted / <u>was painted</u> by my great-grandfather.

  1 **A** What's happened to Shani?

    B She's arrested / 's been arrested.

  2 **A** Was there much damage?

    B The explosion destroyed / was destroyed a lot of buildings.

  3 **A** Were there any casualties?

    B About 50 people injured / were injured.

  4 **A** Have the police got any new information?

    B It appears that they found / were found footprints at the scene of the crime.

  5 **A** Why can't you drive tonight?

    B My car hasn't repaired / hasn't been repaired yet.

7 Complete the news stories. Use the verbs in brackets in the past simple (active or passive), or the present perfect (active or passive).

Two people _have been injured_ in an explosion in a factory. The fire completely ¹ _____ (destroy) the factory and several nearby buildings ² _____ (damage).

A shopkeeper is in hospital in a serious condition after he ³ _____ (rob) last night. The thieves ⁴ _____ (steal) $300 in cash and some cigarettes. The shopkeeper ⁵ _____ (attack) by one of the thieves as he ⁶ _____ (attempt) to stop them.

This week's three-million-pound lottery prize ⁷ _____ (win) by an eighty-six-year-old man. The man, who wishes to remain anonymous, plans to share the money between his five children.

A woman ⁸ _____ (find) guilty of damaging a valuable painting at the City art gallery. The woman ⁹ _____ (claim) in court yesterday that the gallery owed her money. She ¹⁰ _____ (sentence) to a year in jail.

---

natural English
apparently, it appears / seems that

8 Order the words to make sentences.

  A 's / that / hear / I / a bomb/ the city centre / in / gone off

    <u>*I hear that a bomb's gone off in the*</u>

    <u>*city centre*</u> .

  B Oh no.

  A someone / it / seems / a parked car/ left / in / It

    1 _____

    _____ .

  B people / Were / injured / many

    2 _____

    _____ ?

  A no one / appears / hurt / was / It

    3 _____

    _____ .

  A last night / you / the school / hear / robbed / was / that /Did

    4 _____

    _____ ?

  B Really?

  A stole / some kids / a TV / Apparently / and / broke in

    5 _____

    _____ .

expand your grammar

other passive forms

> **Here are examples of the passive in other tenses.**
>
> Present simple passive
> *am / is / are* + past participle
> Most of the parts are imported.
>
> Future simple passive
> *will* + *be* + past participle
> You will be met at the airport by one of our staff.
>
> Present continuous passive
> *am / is / are* + *being* + past participle
> The film is being made in Australia.
>
> Past continuous passive
> *was / were* + *being* + past participle
> Before her death she was being looked after by her daughter at home.
>
> Past perfect passive
> *had* + *been* + past participle
> When they got back from their holiday they discovered that their house had been burgled.

Rewrite the sentences in the passive form. Use *by* + agent only where necessary.

They printed this edition in 2001.
This edition was printed in 2001 .

1 A tall man in a leather jacket was following her.

_____ .

2 We will notify you of your results next week.

_____ .

3 Someone is painting her house this week.

_____ .

4 Someone had already used my credit card by the time I reported it stolen.

_____ .

5 Where do they produce this wine?

_____ ?

 ## how to ... be an ace reporter

natural English getting sb's attention

> **think back!**
>
> Remember four ways of requesting attention.

9 Write questions. Use the words given.

A *Can I ask you something* ? (ask / something)
B OK, if it's quick.

1 A Excuse me, _____ ? (got / moment)
   B Actually I'm running late, sorry.

2 A Sorry to bother you but _____ ? (spare / minute)
   B Sure, what can I do for you?

3 A _____ ? (hurry)
   B A bit, why?
   A I'm doing a survey. Would you answer some questions?
   B Sorry, I'd rather not.

grammar indirect questions

10 Pierre is doing a survey of English-speaking tourists in France. Look at the questions he wants to ask. Complete the indirect questions below.

Where are you from?	5 Do you speak any French?
1 Is this the first time you've been to France?	6 What do you think of French food?
2 How did you get here?	7 How do you feel about French people?
3 How long have you been here?	8 Who is the President of France?
4 Are you by yourself or with a group?	

First of all, could you tell me *where you are from* ?

1 I'd like to know _____ .
2 Could I ask you _____ ?
3 Could you tell me _____ ?
4 I'd like to know _____ .
5 Could I ask you _____ ?
6 I was wondering _____ .
7 I'd be interested to know _____ .
8 Do you know _____ ?

say it!

Imagine that you are going to interview tourists in your country. Ask eight questions, some direct and some indirect. For the indirect questions, use the phrases below to help you.

I'd like to know ...
Could you tell me ... ?
I was wondering ...
I'd be interested to know ...
Do you know ... ?

> Could you tell me what you think of the weather here?

vocabulary expressing opinions and interest

11 Match the beginnings and endings of the sentences.

How do you feel about ... ?

h	I feel
1	I can see
2	I'm not really bothered,
3	I'm not at
4	There's no easy
5	I'm very much
6	It doesn't bother
7	I wouldn't like
8	I'm not all

a all in favour of it.
b against it.
c answer to that.
d to say.
e me that much.
f to be honest.
g both sides.
h ~~quite strongly about that.~~
i that interested in it.

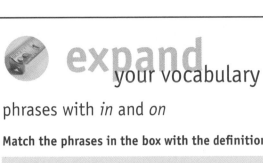

expand your vocabulary

phrases with *in* and *on*

Match the phrases in the box with the definitions below.

| in advance | on a diet | in trouble | on the rise | in depth | ~~in doubt~~ |
| on sale | in pain | in person | on purpose | on behalf of | |

	uncertain	*in doubt*
1	in a detailed and complete way	_____
2	available to buy	_____
3	do sth yourself, face to face (not over the phone or in writing)	_____
4	in a situation that is dangerous or in which you can be criticized or punished	_____
5	trying to lose weight	_____
6	not by accident; deliberately	_____
7	before the time expected or before sth happens	_____
8	increasing	_____
9	as a representative of sb, or instead of sb	_____
10	hurt or ill	_____

Complete the sentences with phrases from the box above.

Next week's show is _in doubt_ if the weather does not get any better.

1 The new album will be _____ from Friday at all good music stores.
2 You have to pay a 10% deposit _____ .
3 I'm here _____ Thomas Mann, who was unable to get here today.
4 She's _____ , but the doctor's giving her something for it.
5 He's _____ with the police again.
6 You can't send her a letter – that's the kind of thing that you have to say _____ .
7 He thinks I did it _____ , but it was just an accident.
8 Recent figures suggest that unemployment is _____ .
9 He studied the contract _____ and decided that it was a good deal.
10 I can't eat chocolate. I'm _____ .

test yourself!

Look at definitions 1 to 10 in the first part above, but cover the phrases on the right. Try to remember the phrases with *in* and *on*.

seven

start off

natural English *what / how / where on earth ... ?*

1 Complete the sentences. Use *on earth* and the words given, in the correct form.

   A I waited for an hour. <u>*Where on earth were you*</u> ?
      (Where / be / you)
   B Sorry! I got held up at work.

1 **A** Sorry I'm late. I missed the bus and had to walk.
   B _____ ? (Why / you / not / call) I could've picked you up!

2 **A** _____ ? (Who / be / that woman)
   B I think it's Sergio's mum. She always wears strange clothes like that.

3 **A** I'll take you to the party but _____ ?
      (how / you / get home)
   B I'm sure someone there will give me a lift back.

4 **A** _____ ? (What / you / do) You're filthy!
   B I've been trying to fix the car.

5 **A** Marta resigned yesterday?
   B _____ ? (Why / she / do /that)
   A She had a row with her boss.

say it!

What would you say in these situations?

Why on earth are they doing that?

Why ... ?   What ... ?

What ... ?   Why ... ?

40

expand your grammar

be supposed to / be expected to

We can use *be supposed to* and *be expected to* to talk about obligation.

be expected to + infinitive

We can use *be expected to* to say what someone should do, either because it is a rule or because someone in authority has said they should do it.

> When a colleague's off sick we're all expected to do their work for them.

> At school we were expected to stand up when the teacher arrived.

The negative form means that sth is not necessary.

> You're not expected to speak fluent English for this position.

be supposed to + infinitive

We can also use *be supposed to* to say what someone should do. We often use it when a rule or an arrangement has already been broken, or may be broken.

> I'm supposed to hand in this essay tomorrow (but I won't have finished it by then).

> I was supposed to be home an hour ago (but I'm late).

The negative form is similar in meaning to *not allowed to*.

> You're not supposed to be in here. It's for first-class passengers only – please leave!

We can also use this form when arrangements have changed or may be changed.

> I was supposed to play tennis with Zac, but we couldn't because of the rain.

Write sentences with the same meaning. Use *be supposed to* or *be expected to*. One or both forms may be possible.

> I told Carlos I'd call him tonight but I forgot.
> I was _supposed to call Carlos tonight but I forgot_ .

1 Do you have to work at the weekends?
Are _____ ?

2 Hurry up! I told Jane we'd pick her up twenty minutes ago!
Hurry up! We _____ !

3 In my last job the boss asked us to do overtime even though we weren't paid for it.
In my last job we _____ .

4 You shouldn't take photos in here.
You _____ .

5 I've arranged to go and visit my grandparents on Sunday but I could go on Saturday instead.
I _____ .

6 You don't have to wear a suit and tie but you should look smart.
You _____ .

7 Do we have to take a present with us to the party tonight?
Are _____ ?

8 I had arranged to have lunch with Marina but she called it off.
I _____ .

say it!

Say sentences using *be supposed to* or *be expected to*.

start work / 9.00 a.m. (expected)
write monthly reports (expected)
work overtime (not expected)
go / meeting yesterday / forgot (supposed to)
use the phone / personal calls (not supposed to)

> I'm expected to start work by 9.00 a.m.

caring for others

grammar present perfect and past simple

2 Underline the correct form. One or both may be possible.

You've written / <u>'ve been writing</u> that letter all day. You must have finished by now.

1 How long has he worked / has he been working there?

2 It's rained / 's been raining for hours. If it doesn't stop soon, there'll be floods.

3 **A** What's all this mess in the kitchen?

B I've cooked / 've been cooking.

4 She's called me / 's been calling me three or four times today.

5 I've worn / 've been wearing contact lenses for ten years.

6 I've read / 've been reading a whole book today!

7 **A** What's the matter?

B I've burnt / 've been burning my finger on the cooker.

8 He's stayed / 's been staying with some friends for the last two months, but now he's got to find his own place.

3 Put the adverbs in the box into the sentences below.

before   yet   never   always   ~~already~~   recently

    already
I've explained it to you three times. Do I need to do it again?

1 I've used this computer program but I'm sure I could get used to it quickly.

2 Have you seen any good films?

3 Haven't you finished that?

4 He's wanted to be a doctor.

5 I don't think we've met, have we?

4 An au pair lives and works with families abroad, looking after the children and usually doing some housework. Carolina has written a letter, applying for an au pair job. Complete the letter. Use the verbs in brackets in the present perfect simple, present perfect continuous, or past simple.

Dear Sir / Madam

I would like to apply for a position as an au pair.

Ever since I <u>was</u> (be) a child, I ¹_____ (always / want) to work with children. I ²_____ (just / leave) school and next year I'm going to do a course in childcare. I'm taking this year off, and would like to go overseas and get some experience that will help me in my studies next year. I ³_____ (not / work) with young children before but my brother has two children, aged two and four. I ⁴_____ (look after) them lots of times.

Last year I ⁵_____ (volunteer) to work in a summer camp with teenagers. I ⁶_____ (be) responsible for organizing sports activities. I ⁷_____ (really / enjoy) it and I'm sure the camp manager would recommend me. I ⁸_____ (also / work) part-time in a shop since last year.

I look forward to hearing from you soon.

Yours faithfully

Carolina Weiss

 write it!

Write a letter of application for a job as an au pair, or as a sports and activities organizer in a children's summer camp. Outline your relevant qualifications, experience and qualities.

natural English degrees of willingness

5 The au pair agency also asks applicants to fill out a form which helps them match au pairs to the most suitable family.

Answer the questions by putting a tick or a cross in the box.

- Would you be willing to

  work in the evenings? ✓

  1 *work at the weekends?* ✗

  2 *do housework?* ✓

  3 *cook meals for the children?* ✓

  4 *look after a baby?* ✗

- Do you have

  5 *a first aid certificate?* ✗

Write Carolina's answers. Use the words given.

willing
I'd be willing to work in the evenings.

1 reluctant _____

_____

2 not mind _____

_____

3 prepared _____

_____

4 find / hard _____

_____

5 no / but / willing / get one _____

_____

say it!

Cover the exercise above. Look at the application form again and answer the questions.

vocabulary volunteer work

think back!

Remember five words connected with volunteer work.

6 Replace the underlined words in the text with words from the box. Keep the meaning the same.

raise	donate	fund-raising events	~~conservation~~	charity

Known worldwide by its panda logo, WWF is the world's largest [1] wildlife and environment protection organization. The WWF works to protect endangered species and habitats around the world. To continue our crucial work, WWF needs help from people like you. Because such a lot of the money we [2] get goes straight into conservation programmes, WWF is one [3] non-profit organization you can trust. When you [4] give money to WWF, you can be assured that your money will be put to immediate use. Or you can help WWF by getting involved in our [5] activities designed to raise money, such as sponsored walks. See our website for this year's events diary.
www.panda.org

1 _conservation_ 　　　　　 4 _____

2 _____ 　　　　　 5 _____

3 _____

vocabulary success and failure

7 Complete each sentence with a word from the box. Change the form of the word if necessary. You do not need to use all of the words.

a success	realize	cope	a fiasco	succeed	~~make~~	handle	do	solve	achieve

Simon is leaving to set up his own computer software company. If anyone can _make_ a success of it, Simon can!

1 How is Paolo _____ with his new job and a new baby?

2 Nicola, there's some confusion over the arrangements for the Christmas party. Will you _____ it for me?

3 Several salesmen have not _____ their targets this month. Perhaps we need to run another training course?

4 The conference last week was _____ . Nothing had been planned properly and everything went wrong.

5 Congratulations to Claire, who has _____ in passing her exams.

wordbooster

conservation

8 Complete the words.

> What's the verb we use when we give food to animals to eat?
> **f** _e_ _e_ _d_

1 What's the adjective for a species of animals that soon may no longer exist?
e _ _ _ _ _ _ _ _

2 What's the word for things like snakes and lizards?
r _ _ _ _ _ _ _

3 What do we say when an animal is kept in a cage?
in c _ _ _ _ _ _ _ _

4 What do we say when an animal is free?
in the w _ _ _

5 What's the verb when archaeologists dig things up?
e _ _ _ _ _ _ _

6 What's another word for the remains of an old building?
r _ _ _ _

7 What's the verb for when we put something under the ground?
b _ _ _

8 What's another word for a historic place?
a historic s _ _ _

uncountable and plural nouns

9 Underline the correct words. Use a dictionary to help you.

> The contents is / <u>are</u> highly toxic.

1 Be careful with that / those scissors.

2 The traffic / traffics seems / seem really bad today, doesn't it / don't they?

3 He gave me some good advice / advices.

4 They used to live on the outskirt / outskirts of town.

5 Have you got any more paper / papers? I need to finish this letter.

6 I've got a lot of experience / experiences in sales.

7 I'm afraid that your luggage / luggages is / are too heavy.

8 Give my regard / regards to Tom.

expand your vocabulary

nouns describing quantity

Read the words and definitions below.

a roll	a long piece of sth that has been wrapped around itself, or around a tube, several times
a pile	a number of things that have been placed on top of each other
a bundle	a number of things tied or wrapped together
a handful	the amount of sth you can hold in one hand
a bunch	a number of things of the same type, which are fastened together or are growing together
a slice	a thin, flat piece of food that has been cut off a larger piece
a spoonful	the amount that a spoon can hold
a sheet	a flat, thin piece of any material, normally square or rectangular
a drop	a very small amount of liquid that forms a round shape

Match the pairs.

_a_	a pile of	a	~~dirty clothes / plates~~
1	a roll of	b	sugar / coffee
2	a sheet of	c	ham / bread
3	a handful of	d	tape / toilet paper
4	a bunch of	e	sand / earth
5	a slice of	f	glass / paper
6	a spoonful of	g	oil / rain
7	a bundle of	h	flowers / bananas
8	a drop of	i	newspapers / firewood

Cover the exercise above. Complete these sentences with a suitable word.

> Have you got another _roll_ of toilet paper?

1 He gave her a big _____ of flowers to apologize.

2 Can I have two _____ of sugar in my coffee?

3 I think I just felt a _____ of rain. Did you bring an umbrella?

4 How many _____ of bread do you want?

5 I've got to do some washing. The _____ of dirty clothes in my bedroom just gets bigger and bigger!

6 Look where you're going! Those men are carrying a _____ of glass.

7 Put in the seeds, then put a _____ of earth over the top.

8 Can you put that _____ of newspapers in the recycling bin?

how to... have a successful interview

natural English putting people at ease

10 Complete the sentences.

Interviewer		Interviewee
Check his name.	It's Thomas, _isn't it_____?	Yes, that's right.
Greet him.	1 It's nice _____.	Nice to meet you too.
Offer to take his jacket.	2 Can _____?	Thanks.
Ask him to sit down.	3 Do have _____.	Thank you.
Ask about his journey to your office.	4 Did you find _____? or	Yes, no problem.
	5 Did you have _____?	No, none at all.

grammar *do, will,* or *would*

11 Write sentences. Use *do / don't, will / won't,* or *would / wouldn't,* and the words given. More than one form may be possible.

  A I'm never going to get everything ready for the party tonight.

  B you / need / help?
      _Do you need some help_____ ?

1 **A** Our dream is to start up our own business one day.

  B you / need / borrow / money?
      _____ ?

2 **A** Can you help us with the move on Sunday?

  B sorry / I / not be able / help
      _____ .

3 **A** Are you going to the shops?

  B Yeah / you / need anything?
      _____ ?

4 **A** I'm going round to Barbara's house.

  B you / give her this book?
      _____ ?

5 **A** I don't think she should take the job they've offered her.

  B No / I / not / take it.
      _____ .

6 **A** My parents are thinking of moving to the country.

  B you / go with them?
      _____ ?

  A No, I don't think so.

7 **A** Don't forget, if you need any help ...

  B I / call you!
      _____ !

8 **A** Can I get you some lunch?

  B No, thanks / I / not feel / hungry
      _____ .

eight

Tick (✓) when you've done these sections.

natural English
- [ ] *all over the ...*
- [ ] making threats
- [ ] apologies and excuses
- [ ] repeated comparatives

grammar
- [ ] verb patterns
- [ ] linking ideas
- [ ] expand your grammar
  ways of adding emphasis

vocabulary
- [ ] expressing anger
- [ ] word building
- [ ] expand your vocabulary
  dealing with problems

natural English *all over the ...*

1 Complete the sentences using a phrase with *all over the ...* . Use the pictures to help you.

He's such a messy eater. There's food *all over the table* .

1 I've looked _____ but I can't find the keys anywhere.

2 He loves travelling. He's been _____ .

3 My sister's got pictures of Enrique Iglesias _____ .

4 She's got jam _____ .

5 There's water _____ . What happened?

say it!

Look at the pictures and say sentences using ... *all over the ...*

There's rubbish all over the lawn.

confrontation

natural English making threats

2 Order the words to make sentences.

me / I / right now / otherwise / shouting / go home / 'll / Stop / at
Stop shouting at me, otherwise I'll go home right now .

1 scream / go / or / 'll / of / my bag / I / Let

_____ .

2 call / otherwise / down / I / Turn / the police / your music / 'll

_____ .

3 or / you / to / help / Listen / won't / me / I / any more

_____ .

4 without / 'll / go / Hurry up / you / I / or

_____ .

5 looking / tell / 'll / my book / I / the teacher / Stop / otherwise / at

_____ .

vocabulary expressing anger

3 Match the beginnings and endings of the sentences.

b	I decided to get my	a	angry very often.
1	We had	b	~~own back.~~
2	He started shouting	c	it irritating.
3	I tried to keep	d	abuse at me in the street.
4	She swore at	e	a huge row.
5	I finally lost	f	with her sister about clothes.
6	She's always quarrelling	g	revenge a few weeks later.
7	It gets on	h	my temper and shouted at him.
8	I don't get	i	her parents, which really upset them.
9	He got his	j	calm, but I was really upset.
10	I find	k	my nerves, but I try to ignore it.

test yourself!

Cover endings a to k and try to finish sentences 1 to 10 from memory.

natural English apologies and excuses

4 Write sentences. Use the words given.

A You've broken my Walkman.
B sorry / I / not / mean / do / it
I'm sorry, I didn't mean to do it .

1 A Hey, be careful – you've spilt your drink on me.
B sorry / I / not / do / it / purpose

_____ .

2 A Why haven't you finished the report yet?
B I / not / aware / it / be / urgent

_____ .

3 A That's my jacket! What are you doing with it?
B I / not / realize / it / belong / you – it was left behind after the party.

_____ .

4 A That wasn't a very nice thing to say.
B I / not / mean / be / rude

_____ .

5 A Hurry up or we'll miss the bus.
B I / not / realize/ you / wait / me

_____ .

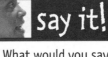

say it!

What would you say in these situations? Use the words given.

I wasn't aware that there was a problem.

Your boss asks you why you haven't dealt with a customer's complaint. It's the first you've heard about the problem. (aware)

You accidentally break a glass. Your friend is really angry about it. (purpose)

You drop in uninvited at a friend's house, but she has dinner guests. (realize)

You say something that upsets a colleague. (mean)

expand your grammar

ways of adding emphasis

The neighbours from hell

Peter and Sally Jones live next door to Karen and Stephen Hansen, who have four dogs. Peter and Sally say that they complained to their neighbours about the barking, and asked them to clean up their backyard because of the smell. They claim that when the noise and smell continued, their only option was to contact the police. The Hansens say that the Jones never spoke to them about the dogs – the first they knew about the problem was when the police knocked on their door. The conflict has got worse since then and the neighbours are no longer talking to each other. Here are some of the statements made by the two couples.

Match pairs of sentences.

Sally Jones	What annoys me most is the noise.	e
Peter Jones	It's the smell that upsets me the most.	1
Sally Jones	What upset us was the fact that they decided to take revenge on us for calling the police.	2
Karen Hansen	It's the fact that they called the police that really upset me.	3
Stephen Hansen	What made matters worse was the fact they were really rude about us to the other neighbours.	4

a They lied about things and tried to make people feel sorry for them.

b I like dogs, but four in an inner city house is too many – it stinks!

c They pulled up our flowers and threw rubbish into our garden.

d Why didn't they just come and have a chat about it first?

e ~~I can't sleep at night because the dogs are always barking.~~

If you want to talk or write about something you feel strongly about, you can use these ways of adding emphasis.

It is / was + noun + *that* + clause
It's the smell that upsets me the most.

It is / was the fact that + clause + *that* + clause
It was the fact that they called the police that really upset me.

What + clause + *is / was* + noun
What annoys me most is the noise.

What + clause + *is / was the fact that* + clause
What upset us was the fact that they decided to take revenge on us.

Rewrite the sentences, making them more emphatic.

He didn't ask me if he could borrow it. That really annoys me.
What *really annoys me is the fact that he didn't ask me if he could borrow it* .

1 I can't stand the noise.
It's _____
_____ .

2 I was most unhappy with the service.
What _____
_____ .

3 He didn't apologize. That made me angry.
It is the fact _____
_____ .

4 He's always late. It really annoys me.
What _____
_____ .

5 The waiter's attitude made things worse.
It was _____
_____ .

 write it!

Write about something that makes you angry or upsets you, or about a confrontation or experience you've had like the one in the story above.

expand your vocabulary

dealing with problems

Match these expressions and definitions.

e	come round
1	talk sth over (with sb)
2	sort sth out
3	have a go at sb
4	have a word with sb
5	talk sb out of (doing) sth
6	talk sb into (doing) sth
7	put up with sth
8	turn a blind eye to sth

a to ignore sth bad that is happening

b to accept sth that is annoying without complaining

c to persuade sb to do sth

d to discuss sth thoroughly, especially in order to reach an agreement or make a decision

e ~~to change your mood or opinion~~

f to deal with a problem in a satisfactory way

g to persuade sb not to do sth

h to speak to sb quickly and briefly

i to criticize sb

Rewrite the underlined parts of the sentences using expressions 1 to 8 above.

Do you think he'll <u>change his opinion</u>?

Do you think he'll _come round_ ?

1 Could I <u>talk to you</u>?

Could I _____ ?

2 I'll <u>ignore it</u> this time, but don't do it again.

I'll _____ this time, but don't do it again.

3 I managed to <u>persuade Yumi to help us</u>.

I managed to _____ .

4 That noisy dog would drive me mad. I don't know how you <u>accept it without complaining</u>.

I don't know how you _____ .

5 We <u>discussed it thoroughly</u> and managed to reach a compromise.

We _____ and managed to reach a compromise.

6 How did you <u>persuade them not to complain</u> to the police?

How did you _____ to the police?

7 I was in a car park this morning when this guy came up and started <u>criticizing me</u>. He claimed that I had taken his parking spot.

I was in a car park this morning when this guy came up and started _____ .

8 It took a long time, but we eventually <u>dealt with it satisfactorily</u>.

It took a long time, but we eventually _____ .

wordbooster

word building

5 **Write sentences with the same meaning. Use the appropriate form of the underlined word.**

The doctor will call you if there's any more <u>deterioration</u> in his condition.

The doctor will call you if his condition _deteriorates_ any more.

1 Have you received any <u>threats</u>?

Has anyone _____ you?

2 Did you agree to <u>compromise</u>?

Did you agree to reach a _____ ?

3 Have you got any <u>proof</u>?

Can you _____ it?

4 Several people have <u>complained</u>.

There have been several _____ .

5 Could you send me a note to <u>remind</u> me?

Could you send me a _____ ?

6 I remember my mum used to give us chocolate when we <u>behaved</u> well.

I remember my mum used to give us chocolate as a reward for good _____ .

7 Is he a <u>suspect</u>?

Do the police _____ him?

8 I'm sure we'll be able to <u>solve</u> it.

I'm sure we'll be able to find a _____ .

too close for comfort

grammar verb patterns

6 Tick the correct forms. One, two, or three may be correct.

Carole has offered
- a to help next weekend. ✓
- b that she buy us dinner.
- c driving me to the station.

1 He denied
- a to break the window.
- b that he was in trouble.
- c stealing the watch.

2 He's going to attempt
- a to climb Mount Everest.
- b that he cross the South Pole.
- c sailing around the world.

3 I suggest
- a to stop soon.
- b that we discuss it with them.
- c take a break for ten minutes.

4 I admit
- a to make a mistake.
- b that I was wrong.
- c told him.

5 He claims
- a to have lots of sales experience.
- b that his dad's a politician.
- c being a law graduate.

6 My boss threatened
- a to cut my pay.
- b that he would fire me.
- c sacking me.

7 I resent
- a to have to pay extra.
- b that I do most of the work.
- c having to work late for no extra pay.

8 Will you promise
- a not to tell her?
- b that you'll be there?
- c being on time?

9 We agreed
- a to discuss it at the next meeting.
- b meeting at 9.00.
- c that it wasn't a very good idea.

10 Do you suspect
- a Tom to do it?
- b that he saw what happened?
- c that he's lying?

7 Complete the text. Use the words in brackets in the correct form. Add any necessary pronouns.

I was amazed when I started my new job. My manager was Cherie, a girl that I'd gone out with at college. She'd been really upset when I broke up with her.

Initially, everything seemed fine. As time went by though, I started to notice that she always asked _me to work_ (work) late in the evenings. The situation took a turn for the worse one evening when we were both working late. She called me into her office and suggested [1] _____ (go) for a drink. I never suspected [2] _____ (still/have) feelings for me so I agreed [3] _____ (go) for one drink. When I stood up to leave she tried to kiss me. When I told [4] _____ (be) married she seemed really embarrassed and made me promise [5] _____ (not/tell) anyone about what she'd done.

Things got much worse at work the next week. She started criticizing my work all the time. She even shouted at me in front of all the staff. The final straw came one afternoon when she threatened [6] _____ (sack) me if I didn't kiss her. I refused and warned her that I was going to report her to the Managing Director for sexual harassment.

When I got to work the next day the Managing Director asked [7] _____ (see) him. Apparently, Cherie was claiming that [8] _____ (**harass**) her. I explained that the situation was actually the other way around, but she denied [9] _____ (try) to kiss me. I tried to persuade [10] _____ (drop) the accusations, but she refused. In the end, I decided to resign. Even now I don't know if she really liked me, or if she just wanted to get revenge for our break-up!

glossary   **harass** /hə'ræs/ to annoy or worry someone by putting pressure on them, or by saying or doing unpleasant things

how to write a letter of complaint

natural English
repeated comparatives

8 Complete the sentences. Use the comparative form of a suitable adjective.

I got _angrier and angrier_ until eventually I went upstairs and told them to shut up.

1 She's getting _____ . Is she on a diet?

2 It became _____ to work and study as well, so I had to drop my course.

3 It got _____ to travel by bus, so I bought a bike. It worked out cheaper in the end.

4 She's getting _____ every day. In fact, the doctors think she'll be able to leave hospital next week.

5 Air travel is getting _____ . Soon we'll be able to fly from London to New York in less than six hours.

say it!

Answer the questions using the adjectives given. Start each sentence with *It's ...* or *I'm getting ...*

You've given up smoking, haven't you? Are you finding it difficult? (easy)

> It's getting easier and easier.

How's your cold? (bad)

Are you still going to the gym every week? (fit)

Are you enjoying your course? (difficult)

grammar linking ideas

9 Write sentences with the same meaning. Use the words given.

The noise gets on my nerves. I can live with it. (although)
Although the noise gets on my nerves, I can live with it .

1 She felt really sick. She carried on working. (despite)
_____ .

2 I asked to see the manager. He wasn't available. (however)
_____ .

3 I apologized. He was still angry. (though)
_____ .

4 There were spelling mistakes. It was a good essay.
(despite) _____ .

5 I told her about it three times. She forgot!
(although) _____ !

6 He didn't do particularly well in the interview. I think we should offer him the job.
(nevertheless) _____ .

7 He had the instructions. He couldn't put it together.
(despite the fact) _____ .

8 There was a delay. We arrived on time.
(in spite of) _____ .

10 Read this extract from a letter of complaint to a restaurant. Complete the letter with suitable link words.

Although we had booked in advance, when we arrived there was no table for us and we had to wait for half an hour. ¹_____ these problems, no one apologized or offered us a drink.

We had asked for a table by the window. ²_____, they finally gave us a table at the back of the restaurant by the kitchen door, where we got hotter and hotter all evening. It took the waiter half an hour to take our food orders, and ³_____ being asked three times, the waiter forgot to bring us our drinks. When the food finally came, we were very disappointed. ⁴_____ that I was extremely hungry, I couldn't eat a thing. The meat was overcooked and cold. My brother said his fish tasted disgusting, and ⁵_____ we had told the waiter that my mother is a vegetarian when we ordered her meal, her pasta had chicken in it.

nine

Tick (✓) when you've done these sections.

natural English
- [ ] expressing great surprise
- [ ] *whenever, wherever*, etc.
- [ ] *the* + comparative, *the* + comparative
- [ ] superlative + *ever*

grammar
- [ ] making comparisons
- [ ] linking words
- [ ] superlatives
- [ ] expand your grammar more linking words

vocabulary
- [ ] books and publishing
- [ ] advertising
- [ ] literal and figurative meaning
- [ ] affixes
- [ ] expand your vocabulary weather words and phrases

start off

vocabulary books and publishing

think back!

Remember five words connected with books and publishing.

1 Fill the gaps with suitable words.

Student	I'm looking for a book. Can you help me?
Shop assistant	What's the _title_ ?
Student	The Oxford Phrasal Verbs Dictionary.
Shop assistant	I don't know it. It must be new.
Student	Yes, I think it only ¹ _____ out a few months ago.
Shop assistant	Who's it ² _____ by?
Student	I'm not sure – maybe Oxford University Press? I know that the front ³ _____ is blue.
Shop assistant	I'll have a look on the computer. OK, I see, it's new. Would you like me to order you a ⁴ _____ ?
Student	Yes please. When will it be here?
Shop Assistant	In about a week. Would you like it in ⁵ _____ or paperback?
Student	Paperback please.

natural English expressing great surprise

2 Write sentences about these situations. Use the words given.

An old friend that you hadn't seen for ten years turned up at your birthday party unexpectedly.
(believe / it) *I couldn't believe it* .

1 You took a day off work and went to the beach, where you bumped into your boss's wife.
(nearly / die) ________________ .

2 You overheard two friends gossiping about your new boyfriend / girlfriend.
(believe / ears) ________________ .

3 You won an award at college for best exam results.
(nearly / faint) ________________ .

4 You saw Madonna in your local supermarket last week.
(believe / eyes) ________________ .

5 You passed an exam that you expected to fail.
(believe it) ________________ .

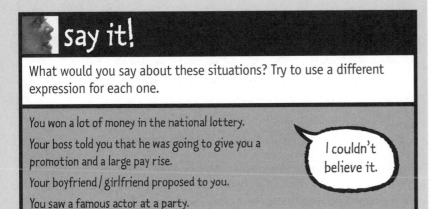

say it!

What would you say about these situations? Try to use a different expression for each one.

You won a lot of money in the national lottery.
Your boss told you that he was going to give you a promotion and a large pay rise.
Your boyfriend / girlfriend proposed to you.
You saw a famous actor at a party.

I couldn't believe it.

making a sales pitch

vocabulary advertising

3 Complete the crossword.

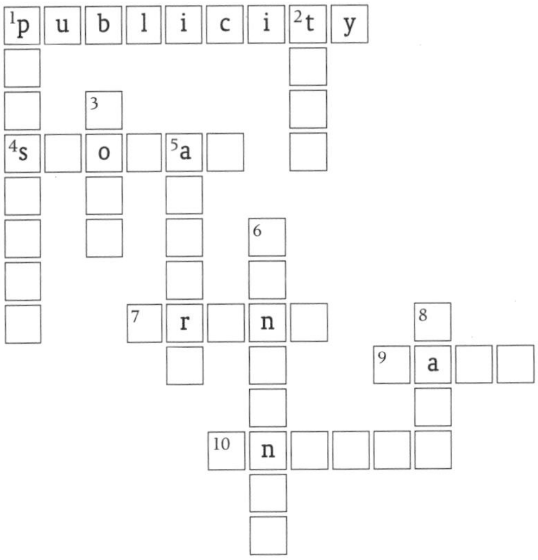

across

1 ~~the attention that is given to sth by newspapers and television~~

4 a memorable word or phrase that's used in advertising to attract attention

7 a type of product made by a particular company; for example a ________ of shampoo

9 has a similar meaning to 7 across; for example a ________ of watch

10 to produce or design something that has not existed before

down

1 to make somebody do something by giving them good reasons for doing it

2 It didn't ________ them very long at all to come up with the idea.

3 a design or symbol that a company uses as its special sign

5 a picture or film designed to inform potential customers about a product

6 another verb with the same meaning as 1 down

8 I have to be home by 9.00. How long does the film ________ ?

natural English
whenever, wherever, etc.

4 Complete the sentences. Use *whenever, whatever, whoever, whichever, wherever* or *however*.

> A I just don't know what to give Karin for her birthday.
> B Why don't you buy her a gift voucher? Then she can get *whatever* she wants.

1 We can go _____ you're ready.

2 I think that _____ team wins today will go on to win the tournament.

3 A You've got some great CDs. Would you mind if I borrowed a couple?
   B No problem, take _____ many you want.

4 Order _____ you want from the menu. It is your birthday after all!

5 Call me _____ you need to. I'll be happy to help if I can.

6 If you need some money, my wallet's on the table. Take _____ much you need.

7 _____ gets the manager's job will have a lot of responsibility.

8 A Where are you going on holiday?
   B I don't know, we haven't decided.
   A Well, have a good time _____ you go!

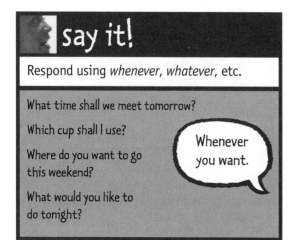

say it!

Respond using *whenever, whatever, etc.*

What time shall we meet tomorrow?

Which cup shall I use?

Where do you want to go this weekend?

What would you like to do tonight?

Whenever you want.

accentuate
the positive

grammar making comparisons

5 Write sentences with the same meaning. Use the words given.

The Shiraz Hotel is the same price as the Welcome Hotel. They are both expensive.
(just) The Welcome Hotel *is just as expensive as the Shiraz* .

1 Her last book was good. So is her latest one.
(just) Her latest book _____ .

2 This flat is double the size of my old one.
(twice) This flat _____ .

3 She used to be a lot quieter than she is now.
(not nearly) She _____ .

4 Driving will only be a bit faster than walking at this time of day.
(nearly) Walking _____ .

5 He's well qualified, and so is she.
(just) She _____ .

6 The Emperor Hotel is much more expensive than the Star.
(not nearly) The Star Hotel _____ .

7 Yesterday's meeting took double the length of time as usual.
(twice) Yesterday's meeting _____ .

8 You've only done a little bit more work than me!
(nearly) I _____ !

write it!

Tom is thinking of buying a new laptop computer. A friend has sent him some information comparing two leading brands, The Studio and The Graphic. Read the e-mail below.

The Studio is supposed to be the best on the market, but to be honest I think the Graphic is just as good and it's nowhere near as expensive. It's nearly as fast as the Studio, but keep in mind that the Graphic is twice as heavy, so it's not as practical if you're travelling a lot.

Write a similar text comparing two products that you are familiar with, for example two mobile phones or two cars.

natural English *the* + comparative, *the* + comparative

6 Complete the sentences. Use the comparative form of the word in brackets.

A Which camera are you going to get?

B This one looks good but it's really expensive.

A Remember *the more expensive* (expensive) it is, *the better* (good) the pictures will be.

1 A It's no good. I really can't do it.

B _____ (hard) you try, _____ (easy) you'll find it.

2 A How are you feeling now? Have you had a rest?

B Yes, but _____ (long) I lie down, _____ (bad) I feel.

3 A Have you told your boss yet that you're leaving?

B No, I'm a bit scared. I think she's going to be really angry!

A _____ (soon) you tell her, _____ (good).

4 A I'll pick you up at 8.00.

B Don't you think that's a bit early.

A _____ (late) we leave, _____ (busy) it'll be.

5 A I'm not sure if I want to go to college. I'd rather just get a job.

B But _____ (good) qualified you are, _____ (money) you're likely to earn.

wordbooster

literal and figurative meaning

7 Complete the sentences with words from the box.

stream	leak	~~deep end~~	depth	wave	flood

They didn't give her any training at all. They just threw her in at the *deep end* .

1 The area has been evacuated and people are now panicking and _____ out of the city in huge numbers.

2 The date and location of the wedding were supposed to be top secret, but details were _____ to the press two hours before.

3 My boss has asked me to give a presentation at the conference but I really don't feel very well qualified to do it. To be honest, I think I'd really be out of my _____

4 Police were unable to prevent hooligans smashing windows and setting light to cars in a _____ of violence after last night's football match.

5 A Have you managed to sell your house yet?

B Not yet, but there's been a steady _____ of people coming to look at it, so we're hopeful.

affixes

think back!

Remember words that use these affixes

-proof   -free   -made   -grown   non-   mini-   multi-   pre-

8 Write words to describe these things, using the affixes above. You may use each affix more than once.

An ice cream that contains no fat. *Fat-free ice cream*

1 A camera that you can use under water. _____

2 Chocolates that are produced by hand. _____

3 Tomatoes you grow in your garden. _____

4 Chewing gum that contains no sugar. _____

5 A **tool** with many different purposes. _____

6 A very small dictionary. _____

7 Paint that is not **toxic**. _____

8 Accommodation that you've booked in advance. _____

Make a list of other words you know that use these affixes.

toxic /ˈtɒksɪk / poisonous

tool /tuːl / a small instrument that you use for making things, repairing things, etc.

how to...
give a successful presentation

grammar linking words

9 Underline the correct option.

A Why does Mr Adamczyk want to have a meeting this afternoon?

B In case / To / <u>So</u> / Otherwise we can talk about the presentations tomorrow.

1 A Why do you need to be at work so early?

B In case / To / So / Otherwise get ready for my presentation.

2 A Why do you need an overhead projector?

B In case / To / So / Otherwise I can illustrate the results of our latest research.

3 A Why are you making so many photocopies?

B In case / To / So / Otherwise any extra people come along.

4 A Make sure you finish the presentation by 10.15 a.m.

B Why?

A In case / To / So / Otherwise there won't be enough time for people to ask questions.

5 A Why did you want to see me so urgently?

B In case / To / So / Otherwise ask for your advice about my presentation today!

say it!

Respond to the questions.

So we don't get stuck in a traffic jam.

Why do you want to leave so early?
So we ...

I tried to call you earlier. Why did you turn your mobile off? So that ...

Why are you taking your jacket?
In case ...

Why are you going to the doctor?
To ...

 # expand
your grammar

more linking words

We can use *as*, *since*, *because* and *because of* to introduce the reason for something.

As and *since* are less common than *because*, and are often used at the start of a sentence.

> As / Since I was already an hour late, I decided not to go.
>
> I decided not to go because I was already an hour late.

Because, *as* and *since* are all followed by a clause.

> Because / As / Since it was raining, we had to cancel the match.

Because of is followed by a noun.

> Because of the rain, we had to cancel the match.

On account of, *owing to* and *due to* are used in the same way as *because of* (they are followed by nouns), but they are more formal.

> All trains will be cancelled tomorrow on account of industrial action.
>
> I must apologize for the delay, which was due to a computer error.
>
> Owing to emergency maintenance work, this office will be closed on Monday.

Complete the sentences. Use suitable link words. More than one answer may be possible.

1 The concert has been cancelled on _account_ of poor ticket sales.

2 The area had to be evacuated _____ to a fire in a nearby chemicals factory.

3 I can't meet you tonight _____ I've got to work late.

4 _____ you've used this computer before, would you mind showing me how it works?

5 _____ to heavy snow, the train has been delayed.

6 The road was closed _____ of floods.

7 On _____ of economic circumstances, we're all going to have to cut our spending.

8 _____ it was your idea, why don't you organize it?

grammar superlatives

10 Write sentences in the superlative. Use the words given.

It / be / tall / building / the world.
It's the tallest building in the world .

1 He / be / good / player / the team.
_____ .

2 Who / be / fluent / speaker / class?
_____ .

3 April / be / wet / month / the year / England.
_____ .

4 She / always / buy / expensive / thing / the shop.
_____ .

5 I / have / bad / time / my life / college / last year.
_____ .

natural English superlative + *ever*

11 Write sentences with the same meaning.

I've never read a better book.
It's the best book I've ever read .

1 I've never seen a taller man.
He's _____ .

2 I've never met anyone more annoying.
He's _____ .

3 I've never been anywhere more interesting.
It's _____ .

4 He's never done anything more difficult.
It's _____ .

5 I haven't seen a better film all year.
That's _____ .

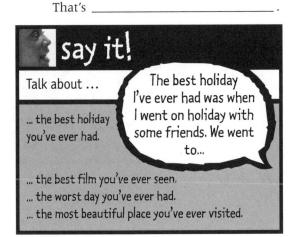

say it!

Talk about ...

> The best holiday I've ever had was when I went on holiday with some friends. We went to...

... the best holiday you've ever had.

... the best film you've ever seen.

... the worst day you've ever had.

... the most beautiful place you've ever visited.

expand your vocabulary

weather words and phrases

Here are some figurative uses of weather words. Match the underlined words and the definitions.

b	He <u>breezed through</u> his exams and got top marks in the class.
1	The thief just <u>breezed into</u> the office, picked up the briefcase, and left. Everyone assumed he worked there!
2	When his boss explained that he would not be getting promoted he <u>stormed out</u>.
3	Pascal and Mustafa still aren't talking to each other, so as you can imagine there was a very <u>frosty atmosphere</u> over dinner.
4	Thanks for the good news. It's really <u>brightened up</u> my day!
5	Try not to let the way he dresses <u>cloud your judgement</u>. He's actually a very good manager.

a when sth happens to make you have a better day
b ~~to do sth successfully and easily~~
c sth that makes it difficult for you to make a good decision
d when a place has an unfriendly feeling because of the people who are there
e to leave a room quickly because you are angry
f to move in a confident and relaxed way

Rewrite the underlined parts of the sentences below. Use a weather word or phrase from above. Keep the meaning the same.

Thanks for the flowers. They <u>made my day much better</u>.
brightened up my day

1 If I'd had to make a speech like that, I would've been really nervous, but he just <u>walked in confidently and calmly</u> and did it.
_____

2 The interview was awful – there was such <u>an unfriendly feeling</u> there.
_____

3 The alcohol probably <u>affected his decision</u>.
_____

4 She <u>found the training easy</u> and now she's ready to start working.
_____

5 They were having an argument when she just <u>left quickly in anger</u>.
_____

ten

start off

vocabulary memory

think back!

Remember five phrases connected with memory.

1 **Complete the responses. Use the words in brackets.**

Do you remember your first day at primary school?
(vague) I've _got a vague memory of it_ .

1 A Have you heard of this company before?
   B (bell) The name _____ .

2 A I won't be surprised if Michael forgets all about it.
   B (minded) Me neither. He's a bit _____ ,
     isn't he?

3 A I can still remember the French national anthem, which we
     learnt in French class at school.
   B (heart) Me too. I _____ .

4 A What's her brother's name?
   B (blank). I can't remember. My _____ .

5 A What's his surname?
   B (tongue) It _____ .

say it!

Reply using one of the memory phrases.

Do you know Simon Hunter?

What's the capital of Bolivia?
Will Ana remember to bring my book?
I'm amazed that you know the words to that song.
Do you remember meeting him a couple of years ago?

> The name rings a bell.

feeling your age

natural English expressions with
tell (recognize)

2 Write sentences with the same meaning.
Use expressions with *tell.*

All types of tea taste the same to me.

I can't _tell one type of tea from another_ .

1 How did you know he was French?

How could you _____

_____ ?

2 I know that one cost a lot more than
the other, but they seem the same to
me.

I know that one cost a lot more than
the other, but I can't _____

_____

between them.

3 Have you seen the twins yet? They look
the same to me.

Have you seen the twins? I can't

_____

the other.

4 As soon as I saw her I knew that
something was wrong.

As soon as I saw her I could

_____ .

5 An Australian and a New Zealand
accent often sound the same to
foreigners.

Foreigners often can't _____
an Australian accent _____
a New Zealand one!

expand your vocabulary

phrases with *age*

Match the underlined words and their meanings.

b		They were buying cigarettes even though they were <u>under age</u>.
1		This wine improves <u>with age</u>.
2		In England you <u>come of age</u> at 18.
3		There was no one there <u>over the age of</u> 15!
4		She married a man <u>twice her age</u>.
5		My grandmother's got very forgetful <u>in her old age</u>.
6		Is there an <u>age limit</u>?
7		She's 30, but she doesn't <u>look her age</u>.
8		Stop being stupid and <u>act your age</u>.

a   you legally become an adult
b   ~~younger than the law allows~~
c   a minimum or maximum age allowed
d   twice as old as her
e   older than
f   appear to be the age she is
g   since she got old
h   behave the age that you are
i   as it gets older

Complete the sentences. Use phrases with the word *age*.

Everyone thinks that he must have married her for her money. She's
twice his age !

1 You shouldn't eat this cheese straight away. It improves

_____ .

2 The boys were thrown out of the bar because they were

_____ .

3 I wish you'd stop being so immature and _____ .

4 In your country is it at 18 or 21 when people _____ ?

5 I always have to carry some ID with me when I go out because
although I'm 25, I don't _____ .

6 My grandfather came to live with us because he found it hard to look
after himself _____ .

7 I must've been the oldest person at the concert. I don't think there
was anyone else _____ 21!

8 Anyone can do the course. There's no _____ .

grammar definite or zero article

3 Add *the* where necessary. More than one *the* may be added in each sentence. Then do the quiz. The answers to the quiz are on *p.63*.

TRIVIA QUIZ

Are these statements true or false?

The   the   the
|Heart is|largest organ in|body.

1 Electric chair was invented by a dentist.

2 Approximately 63,000 trees are used to make Sunday edition of New York Times.

3 Australia is only continent without reptiles or snakes.

4 Approximately 50% of earth is covered with water.

5 Strongest muscle in body is tongue.

6 Neil Armstrong first stepped on moon with his right foot.

7 Average adult is 0.4 inches (1cm) taller in morning than evening, because **spine compresses** during day.

8 Animal responsible for most deaths in world each year is mosquito.

glossary
spine /spaɪn/ the row of small bones that are connected down the middle of the back
compress /kəm'pres/ to press or squeeze together into a smaller space

grammar definite or indefinite article

4 Underline the correct article.

(-) / A / An / The scientists claim that you don't get better at memorizing something just by doing it more. ¹(-) / A / An / The memory just doesn't work that way. But you can get better by learning some clever techniques.

Imagine that you need to buy these things: potatoes, a box of tissues, apples, a box of cornflakes, and some milk. You could invent ²(-) / a / an / the story about how you got some potatoes from ³(-) / a / an / the garden and put them into ⁴(-) / a / an / the large tissue box. While you were doing this ⁵(-) / a / an / the apple fell out of a tree and hit you on ⁶(-) / a / an / the head. And so on, until you have ⁷(-) / a / an / the interesting story that has all the things on ⁸(-) / a / an / the list in it.

Or you could use your imagination to put ⁹(-) / a / an / the things on your list all over your house. For example, think of your sink full of breakfast cereal, with milk pouring out from ¹⁰(-) / a / an / the tap. The funnier the image you create, the more likely you are to remember it.

write it!

A student magazine has invited readers to tell others about how they learn and remember new words. Write a short article for the magazine.

there's no easy answer

vocabulary making judgements

5 Match the texts (a to g) to the headlines (1 to 5).

	Human clone testing given the OK	*e*
1	**Woman, 62, gives birth to twins**	☐
2	**Doctor accused of assisting sick patient to die**	☐ and ☐
3	**GREEN PARK TO MAKE WAY FOR NEW SUPERSTORE**	☐
4	*St Andrew's hospital to close*	☐
5	**Train fares to rise by 20%**	☐

a I've never really thought about that before, but I know that it's <u>something that makes everyone sad</u> when someone is very sick. I guess my feeling is that no one should interfere with life or death.

b Let me think … well, if it happened naturally, then OK, but I think it's ¹ <u>wrong and unacceptable</u> if they used fertility treatment or something like that. She'll be an old woman by the time her kids are in their teens.

c I'll have to think about that for a minute. It's ² <u>against the law</u> in my country, but I know that some doctors have done it. I think in some circumstances ³ <u>there's a good reason for it</u>. If someone is in a lot of pain and they're not going to get any better, ⁴ <u>it causes pain and suffering</u> not to help them if you can.

d I think it's ⁵ <u>a pity</u>. It's a lovely place and lots of people use it. What do we need more shops for?

e That's an interesting question, um … although personally I don't think we should mess around with nature in any way, I do accept that it's ⁶ <u>bound to happen</u>. After all, we've got the technology and it's been done with animals.

f It's ⁷ <u>annoying</u> for me. I have to have medical treatment every two weeks and now I'm going to have to travel to the other side of the city.

g I think it's ⁸ <u>stupid and absurd</u>. Prices are already really high. If they go up any more, it'll be cheaper for me to buy a car and drive to work than get public transport.

Look at the texts again. Match the underlined phrases (1 to 8) to the words in the box below.

a shame	immoral	justifiable
illegal	ridiculous	a nuisance
inevitable	~~upsetting~~	cruel

upsetting

1	_____	5	_____
2	_____	6	_____
3	_____	7	_____
4	_____	8	_____

say it!

What would you say about these situations?

You see a man hitting a dog.

Your flight has been cancelled.

That's cruel.

Some developers are going to knock down a beautiful old building to build a cinema.

The company you work for has been doing badly. They are going to make some staff redundant.

natural English buying time to think

6 Look again at the texts in exercise 5. Find three more phrases that the speakers use to buy time to think, and write them here.

I've never really thought about that before

_____

_____

_____

say it!

Give your opinion. Use the words given.

Is it right to keep animals in captivity? (have to / think)

I'll have to think about that …

What do you think of doctors helping terminally ill patients to die? (never thought)

Do you think human cloning is potentially a good thing? (interesting question)

Do you think parents should have the right to choose the sex of their baby? (let / think)

wordbooster

animals

think back!

Remember five words connected with animals.

7 Complete the sentences with a suitable word.

Amazing animal facts

The Inland Taipan, an extremely poisonous snake, has enough venom in one _bite_ to kill more than 200,000 mice.

1 Since domestic cats are clean, with dry and glossy coats, their _____ can become charged with electricity. Sparks can be seen if they are stroked in the dark.

2 The hippopotamus has _____ that is an inch and a half thick. It's so solid that most bullets cannot penetrate it.

3 No two zebra have the same pattern of _____ .

4 It is usually the female lion who _____ for food, while the male prefers to rest.

5 Elephants perform greeting ceremonies when a member of the _____ returns after being away for some time.

6 The Egyptian vulture, a large white bird, throws stones with its _____ to open ostrich eggs to eat.

7 The round or oval _____ on an adult cheetah can measure up to 1.5 inches in diameter.

8 In the USA each year more people die from scorpion _____ than snakebites.

word building

8 Complete the sentences. Use the words given, in the correct form.

Perhaps they'll agree after a bit of _persuasion_ . PERSUADE

1 I don't like to see animals in _____ . CAPTIVE

2 Some people think it's _____ to keep birds in cages. CRUELTY

3 I don't think there's any _____ for what he did. JUSTIFY

4 You need to show a lot of _____ in this kind of work. SENSITIVE

5 The meeting was very _____ . CONSTRUCTION

6 Her behaviour was _____ . DISGRACE

7 The cyclone caused widespread _____ . DESTROY

8 He's quite _____ . He makes a lot of mistakes in his work. CAREFUL

how to
write a

grammar relative clauses

9 Complete the sentences. Use relative pronouns (*that, which, who, whose*). If it is possible to omit the pronoun, do not write anything.

Only pack the things _that_ are absolutely necessary.

1 The medicine _____ she's taking doesn't seem to be having any effect.

2 The room was full of students _____ were waiting to take a test.

3 I've just seen someone _____ I used to go to school with.

4 His first book, _____ he wrote when he was 20, has now been translated into ten different languages.

5 The painting _____ was stolen from the gallery is said to be worth a fortune.

6 The woman _____ children I look after has had plastic surgery.

7 I think people _____ have plastic surgery often look worse afterwards!

8 The operation, _____ lasted for six hours, was successful.

10 Add commas, if necessary.

My sister Jane, who lives in Australia, has just had a baby.

1 The waiter who served us was very rude.

2 He sold his car which is the same as mine for $5000.

3 That's the woman who's just taken over as manager.

4 Can you give me back the money I lent you yesterday?

5 His boss who's a workaholic insists that they all work late.

6 Our hotel room which obviously hadn't been cleaned for days was awful.

7 The man I spoke to on the phone said that we didn't need to make reservations.

8 My boss who lives in my street gave me a lift home.

human interest story

11 Combine the sentences to make one sentence. Start with the words given.

How is the man? He was injured in the accident.

How is the man who was injured in
the accident ?

1 I had an argument with the manager. He refused to exchange a pair of shoes. I'd bought the shoes the week before.

I had an argument with the manager
_____
_____ .

2 You gave me a book. I lent it to my brother. He lost it.

I lent the _____
_____ .

3 I gave you a phone number yesterday. It was wrong.

The phone number _____
_____ .

4 My older brother is a lawyer. He might be able to help you.

My older brother _____
_____ .

5 Do you know the boy? His bike was stolen.

Do you _____
_____ ?

expand your grammar

participle clauses

When a participle comes after a noun, it gives more information about the noun.

Who's that boy <u>standing</u> outside the house?

I don't know the man <u>sitting</u> over there.

Participle clauses often have the same function as relative clauses.

Do you know the man <u>getting</u> (= who's getting) out of the blue car?

The medication <u>prescribed</u> (= that was prescribed) by my doctor is very expensive.

Change these relative clauses into participle clauses.

Staff ~~who are~~ working on the second floor will have to use the stairs.

1 Fish which is caught off the north coast is sold in the cities in the south.

2 The girl who's going out with my brother is a nurse.

3 The film that's showing at the moment is new.

4 Their latest record, which was released two days ago, has gone straight to the top of the charts.

5 Did you see a man who was running out of that shop?

Make one sentence, using a participle clause.

A girl is staying with us at the moment. She's French.

The girl staying with us at the moment is French .

1 A man was arrested by the police yesterday. He has been charged with murder.

The man _____ .

2 Do you recognize the man? He is talking to Joe.

Do you recognize the man _____ ?

3 Some people were interviewed today. None of them were offered the job.

None of the people _____ .

4 A woman is walking towards us. She's Sam's girlfriend.

The woman _____ .

5 The diamond was stolen from the museum in 1980. It has never been recovered.

The diamond _____ .

eleven

Tick (✓) when you've done these sections.

natural English
- [ ] exaggerating
- [ ] letter writing clichés
- [ ] reacting to ideas
- [ ] informal and formal language

grammar
- [ ] past conditionals
- [ ] past and mixed conditionals
- [ ] reporting what people say
- [ ] expand your grammar *it's time* ...

vocabulary
- [ ] describing character
- [ ] phrases and phrasal verbs
- [ ] expand your vocabulary crimes

start off

natural English exaggerating

1 Complete the sentences so that the meaning is more exaggerated.

I'm really busy.
I've got _a million things to do_ .

1 It's very heavy.
It weighs _____ .

2 It was very expensive.
It cost _____ .

3 I'm starving.
I could eat _____ .

4 I'd never do that.
I wouldn't do that in _____ .

5 I've already told you lots of times.
I've told you _____ .

say it!

Say the sentences below and add one of the phrases above.

Don't just turn the computer off. You have to shut it down first.

Have you got anything to eat?
Can you help me lift this case?
I can't believe she's going paragliding!
I can't believe they bought it for me.

> I've told you a hundred times to shut it down before you turn it off.

making the right decision

grammar past conditionals

2 What would you say in these situations? Use the verbs given in the correct form.

A relative who is coming to stay with you arrives exhausted at your house. He has walked from the station.

If you *'d called* (call), I *would've picked you up* (pick you up).

1 You left home late. You missed the bus.

If we _____ (leave) earlier, we _____ (not/ miss) the bus.

2 Your friend didn't tell you about her birthday party until the day before, so you couldn't take the evening off work.

I _____ (take) the evening off work if you _____ (tell) me about it sooner.

3 You are at a party. A friend arrives at 9.30. Another old friend, Johan, left the party at 8.30.

If you _____ (get) here an hour ago, you _____ (see) Johan.

4 A friend told you something but didn't tell you it was a secret. You told someone else. Now your friend's angry with you.

If you _____ (say) it was a secret, I _____ (not/ tell) anyone.

5 You and your sister are going to visit a friend. Your sister left the map at home and you are now lost.

We _____ (be) there hours ago if you _____ (not/ leave) the map at home.

grammar past and mixed conditionals

3 Underline the correct form.

Juan   I'm so sorry that there was no one waiting at the airport to meet you.

Ana   No problem – I got a taxi.

Juan   If I'd had your flight details I would pick you up / <u>would've picked you up</u> myself.

Lina   Thanks for helping me with that essay.

Yuri   That's OK.

Lina   I ¹wouldn't finish / wouldn't have finished it on time if you hadn't helped me. In fact I think I ²'d be working / 'd have worked on it now!

Eva   I can't believe you forgot to book the holiday.

Adam   Well, that's not my fault, is it? You were supposed to book it.

Eva   I was too busy.

Adam   If you'd told me that, I ³could do / could've done it myself.

Eva   Well, it's too late now, isn't it?

Adam   There are still some tickets left but it's expensive. If we'd booked it last week it ⁴would be / would've been much cheaper – now the tickets are almost double the price.

Eva   I don't think we can afford it, do you?

Adam   No, not after you spent all that money on your motorbike. If you hadn't spent so much we ⁵would have / would've had plenty of money now.

4 Complete the sentences. Use the words in brackets in the correct form, with *would* or *might*. Both *would* and *might* may be possible.

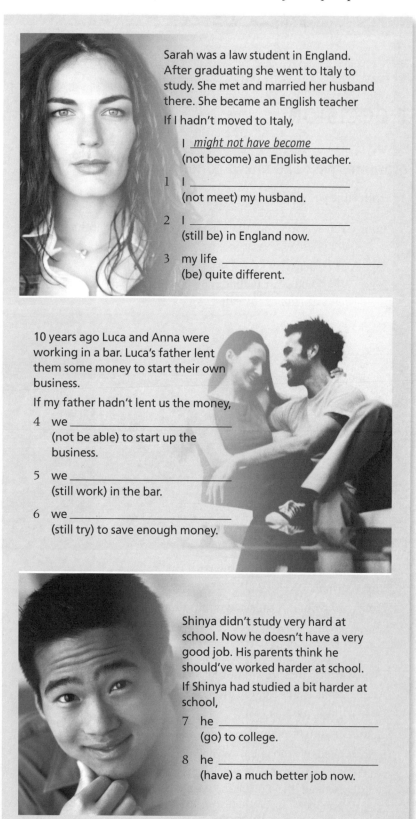

Sarah was a law student in England. After graduating she went to Italy to study. She met and married her husband there. She became an English teacher

If I hadn't moved to Italy,

I _might not have become_ (not become) an English teacher.

1 I _____ (not meet) my husband.

2 I _____ (still be) in England now.

3 my life _____ (be) quite different.

10 years ago Luca and Anna were working in a bar. Luca's father lent them some money to start their own business.

If my father hadn't lent us the money,

4 we _____ (not be able) to start up the business.

5 we _____ (still work) in the bar.

6 we _____ (still try) to save enough money.

Shinya didn't study very hard at school. Now he doesn't have a very good job. His parents think he should've worked harder at school.

If Shinya had studied a bit harder at school,

7 he _____ (go) to college.

8 he _____ (have) a much better job now.

Now think of something that happened to you in the past. Write three sentences about it, like the sentences above.

wordbooster

phrases and phrasal verbs

think back!

Remember the meanings of these phrases and phrasal verbs.

end up doing sth	cover sth up
put up with sth	confide in sb
ashamed of sth /sb	out of the blue
by mistake	~~get mixed up with sb~~
turn up	

5 Complete the sentences. Use the verbs and phrases above, in the correct form.

She _got mixed up with_ some older girls who were shoplifting.

1 We waited for the bus for 40 minutes but eventually _____ getting a taxi.

2 They'd only met once, about a year before, but he called her _____ and asked her out.

3 They _____ at the restaurant late and Dad was really angry with them.

4 Sorry, I took your book _____ yesterday.

5 Something's wrong with Akiko. Could you have a chat with her? Maybe she'll _____ you.

6 The traffic noise here is awful. How do you _____ it?

7 The policemen who interviewed him think he's trying to _____ something _____ .

8 She's _____ the way she behaved when she met you last time. She was really nervous and it made her behave stupidly.

expand your vocabulary

crimes

Match the words in the box to the sentences.

assault	vandalism	rape
mugging	hooliganism	~~shoplifting~~
fraud	burglary	drug dealing

A woman stole some make-up from a department store. _shoplifting_

1 A man threatened an elderly woman and took her bag. _____

2 A man forced a woman to have sex with him. _____

3 A woman broke into a house and stole money and goods. _____

4 A man smashed the windows of a shop and sprayed paint all over a wall.
_____

5 A woman was the director of a company. She arranged for company money to be transferred to her own bank account.
_____

6 A man badly injured another man during a fight. _____

7 A woman sold drugs. _____

8 A man joined other fans in rioting after a football match. _____

test yourself!

Look at the pictures. What crimes are being committed?

a time to forgive

natural English letter writing clichés

6 Complete the letter with suitable phrases.

Dear Alison,

Hi. I hope _you're well_ . Sorry I haven't written
1 _____ but I've been very busy at college with my final
exams. They're all over now thank goodness! Thanks for my birthday
card – it was lovely to hear 2 _____ and get all of your
news. I was so 3 _____ that you managed to find a
new job. I know how unhappy you were in your last one. Now I guess
I'll have to start looking for work soon...

write it!

Imagine that you have just received a letter from an English-speaking friend, telling you some good news. The last time you wrote to this friend was six months ago. Write back to your friend.

vocabulary describing character

7 Underline the most suitable word.

Be careful what you say to her. She's feeling full of remorse / <u>vulnerable</u> / naive after her illness.

1 When my mum died my boss encouraged me to take some time off work. He was very understanding / sincere / open-minded.

2 Don't believe a word he tells you. He's completely reckless / untrustworthy / naive.

3 I think it would be unwise / vulnerable / brave to invest any more money in that company – they're doing very badly.

4 My grandmother is the most open-minded / naive / kind-hearted person I know. She'll do almost anything for anyone.

5 She's so naive / trustworthy / understanding that she believed him when he told her that he was a member of the royal family.

6 He comes across as being quite sincere / wise / easily led, but in fact he's a liar and a cheat.

7 I think that people in my country are fairly kind-hearted / vulnerable / open-minded about couples living together before they get married.

8 After the accident he was arrested for courageous / reckless / unwise driving.

expand your grammar

it's time ...

> **We use the structure _it's time_ + clause to say what we think should happen soon or what someone should do soon.**
>
> It's time we left. = We should leave now.
>
> It's time you got a haircut. = You should get your hair cut.
>
> **Notice the tense of the verbs in the examples. We use the past tense to express a hypothetical situation. This is sometimes called the unreal past.**
>
> It's time he <u>started</u> looking for a job.
>
> It's time the government <u>spent</u> some money on education.

Complete the sentences. Use the words given in the correct form.

You look really run down. (time / you / have) _It's time you had_ a holiday.

1 I can't believe you two are still not talking to each other. Don't you think (time / you / apologize) _____ ?

2 I've put on a lot of weight recently. (time / I / go) _____ on a diet.

3 The health system is terrible. (time / the government / do) _____ something about it.

4 He's been missing for 24 hours. (time / we / call) _____ the police.

5 I've got my exams in two weeks' time. (time / I / start) _____ doing some revision.

6 He's been working there for four years. I think (time / they / give) _____ him a pay rise.

7 My dad's over 65. (time / he / retire) _____ but he doesn't really want to.

8 You've been working on the computer for ages. (time / you / take) _____ a break.

natural English reacting to ideas

8 Put sentences a to d into the text.

a I'm completely against it.

b It sounds like an interesting idea,

c I've got mixed feelings about it.

d ~~I'm totally in favour of the idea.~~

HAVE YOUR SAY!

> 66 If teenagers under the age of 16 had to be home by 9.00 p.m., or else the police could arrest them, it would prevent a lot of kids from getting involved in crime. 99

Alicia   _d_ I think it would make a big difference if teenagers weren't allowed to be out on the streets at night. If they're at home with their parents there's no way they can get into trouble.

Kosuke   [1] ___ but I'm just not sure that it would work. It would depend very much on the parents and how well they could control their children, don't you think?

Alicia   Yes, but then it should be the responsibility of the parents and not the police anyway. What do you think Iwona?

Iwona   [2] ___ A lot of kids would absolutely hate it because it would mean they couldn't just **hang out** with their friends in the evening. And I think that the real troublemakers would **sneak out** of the house anyway!

Alicia   But if the police arrest them, or take them home, then that might prevent them from causing trouble.

Kosuke   That's true.

Thiago   I don't know – [3] ___ On the one hand it might stop some teenagers getting into trouble. On the other hand, some innocent kids might get picked up by the police.

---

glossary

sneak out /sniːk aʊt / to leave secretly

hang out /hæŋ aʊt / spend time together

---

say it!

Say phrases using the words given.

mixed feelings
against
favour
interesting

> I've got mixed feelings about it.

Give your real opinion on the subject in the dialogue above.

how to... write an apology

grammar reporting what people say

9 Match sentences a to g to the pictures.

Later, Tom tells his story to a friend. Put Tom's story into reported speech. Use the direct speech in the pictures to help you.

> We had arranged to go to the cinema. At about 6.00 she rang and said _she couldn't see me that night_ . She explained that
> 1 _____ late. I decided to go and see the film anyway. As I was going into the cinema, I caught sight of her going into a restaurant further down the road. She was with another man. I decided to call her mobile and I asked her where she was. She said
> 2 _____ work. I suggested meeting for coffee afterwards but she said 3 _____ 10.00 and that
> 4 _____ to meet me then. So, later that night I decided to go round to her house but she wasn't home yet. I left her a message to meet me the next day at the café we usually go to. When we met I told her 5 _____ . She explained that
> 6 _____ to get something to eat. I asked her about the man and she said 7 _____ . I told her
> 8 _____ , and she stormed out. I haven't seen her since then, and she's not answering her phone.

say it!

Report an argument that you've had with someone recently.

natural English informal and formal language

10 Read Julie's e-mail to Tom. Underline the most informal phrases.

> Dear Tom
>
> I really must apologize for / <u>I'm really sorry about</u> walking off earlier, but you weren't listening to me – you were so angry! But you were right – I did lie to you and there's something I have to tell you.
> 1 It's about / It's regarding the man you saw me with. He's my ex-boyfriend. He rang me last week and said that he was still upset about our break-up and he really wanted to talk things over. I felt sorry for him – that's the only reason I agreed to meet him. I didn't mean to upset you. 2 It's all my fault / I accept full responsibility – I should've told you the truth. Will you ever forgive me? Please 3 contact / ring me.
>
> Love
> Julie

a Julie walked off.

b Later that evening he went to Julie's house but there were no lights on.

c The next day Tom met Julie in a café. He confronted her and they had a row.

d On the way, he saw Julie sitting in a restaurant with another man.

e Tom went to the cinema on his own.

1 f ~~Julie cancelled her date with Tom.~~

g Eventually Tom decided to call Julie but she lied to him about where she was.

twelve

start off

vocabulary times of day and sleep

think back!

Remember three words connected with times of the day and three words connected with being asleep.

1 Complete the sentences with a suitable word.

I went to bed at 11.00 p.m., but it was probably midnight before I finally fell _asleep_ .

1 It was 4.30 a.m. by the time the party finished, so we stayed up and sat on the beach to watch the _____ . It was very romantic.

2 They're building a new apartment block next door to us, so it's noisy from _____ to _____ .

3 There's no point in going to bed yet – I'm still _____ awake.

4 Why don't you have a _____ ? You might feel better when you wake up.

5 He suffers from _____ . Some nights he can't sleep at all.

6 I've tried to wake her up but she's _____ asleep.

7 His teachers say that he would do much better at school if he stopped _____ about things in class.

8 My husband _____ loudly. Sometimes it's so bad that I have to sleep in another room.

questions!
questions!

natural English phrases with *mean*

2 Complete the sentences. Use a phrase with *mean*.

Do you know somebody called Francesca DiNapoli? No, sorry, the name doesn't
mean anything to me .

1 Someone rang from a company called Hydrogel. Does the name
_____ ?

2 He doesn't care about the salary. He says that money
_____ .

3 Thanks for going to Dad's party. I know it _____ .

4 Have a look at this symbol. What does _____ ?

5 Please be careful with that vase – it belonged to my grandmother so it
_____ .

say it!

Rephrase the sentences. Use a phrase with *mean*.

The watch that was stolen meant a lot to me.

The watch that was stolen was very important to me.

What do you understand by FR2?

Do you know who Enrique Alfonso is?

Job satisfaction is important to me.

grammar reported questions

3 Anders recently arrived in the USA. The immigration officer at the airport asked him a lot of questions.

Read their conversation below.

IO What's your full name?
A Anders Henry Jacobson.
IO [1] Are you here on holiday, Anders?
A No, I'm going to study English.
IO I see. [2] How long are you planning to stay?
A Two months.
IO [3] Do you know anyone in the USA?
A I've got an aunt who lives here.
IO Really? [4] Where does your aunt live?
A Chicago.
IO And are you going to stay with her?
A I might visit her later.
IO [5] Where are you going to stay in New York?
A With a homestay family.
IO OK. [6] How much money do you have with you?
A I've got $500 in cash and a credit card.
IO [7] Have you been to the USA before?
A Yes – a couple of years ago.
IO And [8] what did you do then?
A I was on holiday with my family.

Anders is telling his host family in the USA about his conversation with the immigration officer. Report the officer's questions.

She asked *me what my full name was* .

1 She wanted to know _____ .
2 She asked me _____ .
3 She wanted to know _____ .
4 She asked me _____ .
5 She wanted to know _____ .
6 She asked me _____ .
7 She wanted to know _____ .
8 She asked me _____ .

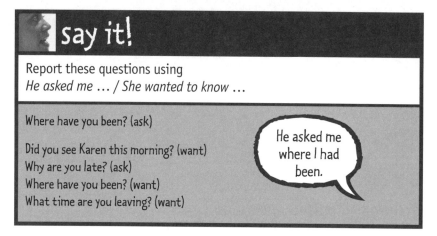

say it!

Report these questions using
He asked me ... / She wanted to know ...

Where have you been? (ask)

Did you see Karen this morning? (want)

Why are you late? (ask)

Where have you been? (want)

What time are you leaving? (want)

> He asked me where I had been.

natural English phrases with *go*

4 Order the underlined words to make phrases.

A I've got a headache.

B Dissolve one of these tablets in water. It tastes disgusting, so
all / go / drink / in / it / one

  drink it all in one go .

1 A I'm just going to the toilet.

B Don't be long. 's / your / next / go / It

  _____ .

2 A I've been offered promotion but I'm a bit nervous about accepting it. It's going to be hard.

B should / it / I / for / go / think / you

  _____ .

3 A I don't understand how this thing fits together and there aren't any instructions.

B go / Let / have / me / a

  _____ .

attitude adverbs

5 Match the pairs of sentences, and choose an adverb to join each sentence. More than one adverb may be possible.

funnily enough	miraculously	presumably
hopefully	understandably	surprisingly
~~predictably~~	luckily	obviously

| h | We arranged to meet at 8.00 but *predictably* ... |

1 ☐ We're hoping to set up our own business but _____ ...

2 ☐ I thought that it was going to be really boring, but
  _____ ...

3 ☐ I lost my passport but
  _____ ...

4 ☐ They haven't responded to the invitation so _____ ...

5 ☐ He wasn't offered the job so
  _____ ...

6 ☐ We haven't found a flat to rent yet but _____ ...

7 ☐ The hotel was cheap so we were expecting it to be run-down, but
  _____ ...

8 ☐ It started raining the moment we got there but _____ ...

a ... they're not coming to the wedding.

b ... someone had a spare umbrella.

c ... he's very disappointed.

d ... I quite enjoyed it.

e ... we'll need to get a loan from the bank.

f ... it was really quite luxurious.

g ... someone handed it in to the police.

h ... ~~he turned up late. I don't think he's ever been on time.~~

i ... we'll have found one by Christmas.

collective nouns

6 Underline the correct word.

He's written a set / pile / <u>series</u> of books about learning and teaching languages.

1 Police suspect a herd / gang / set of local boys of vandalizing the shop.

2 The jury / public / congregation were unable to agree on a verdict in the murder trial.

3 If you want something to read, there's a set / pile / series of magazines on the coffee table.

4 My sister sings in her school congregation / choir / jury.

5 The crowd / audience / public waiting outside the band's hotel was so big that the police were called to control them.

6 Fortunately the staff / jury / crew of the sinking ship were rescued.

7 The children were making so much noise it sounded like there was a herd / gang / set of elephants in the next room.

8 Have you got a pile / set / series of playing cards?

test yourself!

What can you see in these pictures?
Write a collective noun next to each one.

a herd of cows _____

_____ _____

boost your brain power

natural English rephrasing an idea

7 Put these sentences into the dialogues.

a ~~I'll probably fail~~

b that I shouldn't get my hopes up

c that I shouldn't drive, or anything like that, after I've taken them

d you don't like my idea

e that you want to break up with me

f that it makes me look fat

A If you really want to pass this exam, you're going to have to do a lot of work for it.

B So what you're trying to say is that _a_ .

A Well there's a chance you could pass, but only if you start studying a lot harder.

1 A I think there may be other options that we haven't considered yet.

B So what you mean is ___ .

A No, I just think that we shouldn't make a quick decision.

2 A Remember that they've probably had over 200 applications for the job.

B So what you're trying to say is ___ .

A Well, you've got a good chance, but don't be too disappointed if you don't get it.

3 A Maybe we should both start going out with other people a bit more often, you know, not see each other every night.

B So what you mean is ___ .

A No, that's not what I said. It's just that I don't see my old friends very much at the moment.

4 A It's a nice dress but it looks a bit small on you.

B So what you're saying is ___ .

A Um … to be honest, yes.

5 A There can be some side effects from taking this medication, such as drowsiness.

B So what you're saying is ___ .

A That's right, yes.

grammar *like, as, such as*

8 Complete the sentences. Use *like* or *as*.

I'm hoping to get a job _as_ a chef.

1 I think he's very much _____ his father.

2 I eat a lot of dairy food _____ cheese and yogurt.

3 The kidnappers told him to do _____ they said and everything would be OK.

4 Don't you think this sauce smells _____ rotten fish? It's disgusting.

5 We'd like to go on honeymoon to somewhere romantic _____ France or Italy.

6 _____ I explained to you earlier, I'm afraid there's nothing we can do about the delay.

7 Martin always uses a headache _____ an excuse to take the day off work.

8 She's just started working _____ a nurse.

9 She says her dad still treats her _____ a child even though she's 15.

10 Critics have described the film _____ the best they've seen in the last year.

In which of the sentences above is *such as* possible?

say it!

Say these sentences using *as*, *like* or *such as*.

He's exactly / his dad.

He likes spicy food / Thai and Indian.

We had to use my shoe / a hammer.

She looks a bit / Gwyneth Paltrow.

He's just started work / a teacher.

> He's exactly like his dad.

expand *your vocabulary*

thinking and the brain

Maximize your brainpower!

Everyone has experienced days when they seem to be <u>functioning</u> better than usual; they can think quickly, and concentration and problem solving seem easy. Unfortunately, everyone has also had days when the opposite is true; it's difficult to <u>focus</u>, <u>distractions</u> are everywhere, and even the smallest <u>mental task</u> is a challenge. What can help you to increase the number of days in the first category?

Practice: Some studies have suggested that a person can improve his or her ability by <u>visualizing</u> themselves performing, playing Beethoven sonatas or a game of chess in the imagination for example.

Emotions: Negative thoughts can make you anxious and cause you to lose concentration. If you <u>have something on your mind</u> it can really disrupt your thinking. Try to <u>clear your head</u> and stay positive and you'll perform well.

Music: Fast music with a heavy beat can be <u>stimulating</u>, while other music may aid relaxation.

Find underlined words in the text that mean:

to empty your mind of thoughts _to clear your head_

1 a particular activity that involves a lot of thinking _____

2 make the best use of sth _____

3 give attention to one particular subject, situation or person _____

4 forming a picture of something in your mind _____

5 working in the correct way _____

6 making people enthusiastic / making the brain more active _____

7 be worried about something _____

8 things that take your attention away from what you are doing _____

Complete the sentences. Use words from the text in the correct form.

I can't do any _mental tasks_ , like studying, at night.

1 If I have to give a presentation I usually _____ myself doing it first, and that seems to help.

2 I'm not a morning person! My brain just doesn't _____ until after 11.00 a.m.

3 I love playing chess. I find it really _____ .

4 I find it really hard to _____ on things if I'm tired.

5 If I _____ , I just can't concentrate. I have to sort out the problem first, and then get to work.

6 Unfortunately, if there are any _____ while I'm working, I find it impossible to concentrate.

7 I try to _____ my time in the mornings because that's when my brain works best!

8 I have to _____ of everything else before I start a task – I just can't think about more than one thing at a time.

how to
explain the rules of a game

natural English saying how easy something is

9 Complete the words.

It's e _a_ _s_ _y_ .

1 It's not hard at all. In fact it's
s _ _ _ _ g _ _ f _ _ _ _ _ d.

2 It's easy once you get the **h _ _ _** of it.

3 It's quite **c _ _ p _ _ _ _ t _ _**. You need to follow the instructions carefully.

4 The instructions are hard to
f _ _ _ _ w.

5 It's really **s _ _ _ l _** . I did it easily.

vocabulary games

think back!

Remember five words connected with playing games.

10 Complete the sentences. Use the verbs in the box in the correct form.

| win | give | be | take | guess |
| ~~have~~ | compete | miss | throw | |

Even if you're not sure, you should
have a guess.

1 On that game show several families _____ against each other.

2 Everyone _____ the dice and the person with the highest number then starts the game.

3 What sort of prizes do people _____ on that show?

4 If you get the question wrong, you have to _____ a turn.

5 You _____ it in turns to make a word.

6 The person with the lowest score in each round _____ out.

7 You have to _____ what card I'm holding.

8 Do you need some help? Do you want me to _____ you a clue?

expand
your grammar

question word clauses

Look at the phrases below, which can be used to say that you don't know or are not sure about something.

<u>I've got no idea</u> what the answer is.

<u>I haven't got a clue</u> who invented it.

<u>I don't know</u> whose go it is next.

<u>I'm not sure</u> if this answer is correct.

<u>I can't remember</u> when that happened.

Notice the word order. It is the same as for indirect questions.

With *wh-* questions, the main verb comes after the subject (i.e. positive word order).

What's the answer?

<u>I've got no idea</u> what the answer is.

The auxiliary verbs *do / does / did* are not used.

Where does he live?

<u>I haven't got a clue</u> where he lives.

With *yes / no* questions, we use *if* or *whether* + subject + verb.

Is this answer correct?

<u>I'm not sure</u> if this answer is correct.

Does she like that kind of thing?

<u>I'm not sure</u> whether she likes that kind of thing.

Complete the sentences. Use the direct questions in brackets to help you.

(Where did we stay?) I can't remember _where we stayed_ . It was a long time ago.

1 (What will he say?) I've got no idea _____ , but ask him anyway.

2 (Why am I so tired?) I don't know _____ . I went to bed at 9.00 p.m. last night!

3 (What time does the film start?) I'm not sure _____ . Can you check?

4 (Where are we?) I haven't got a clue _____ . Will you have a look at the map?

5 (Does Judy want to come with us?) I'm not sure _____ . Ask her!

6 (Where has Mayumi gone?) I don't know _____ .

7 (How long will it take?) I've got no idea _____ , so we'd better leave early.

8 (Where did I put my keys?) I can't remember _____ .

unit one

1 1 f, 2 d, 3 c, 4 a, 5 e

say it *Students' own answers.*

2 1 Do you play a lot of sport?
2 We don't watch much TV.
3 He *doesn't do any / does no* exercise at all.
4 We go skiing a lot in the winter.
5 I haven't done much revision for my exams.

3 1 I found it hard to understand the listening test.
2 I found the vocabulary test tricky.
3 Describing the pictures was the hardest part.
4 I was hopeless at the grammar test.
5 I found the writing test quite challenging.

say it I found the vocabulary test challenging.
I found it hard to finish the reading test
in time.
I was hopeless at the speaking test.
I found the grammar test quite tricky.

4 1 a magazine / a grammar book
2 news / fashion / technology
3 know / learn
4 a few pages / class / lunch
5 get

5 1 going, 2 went, 3 join, 4 practise, 5 taken, 6 won,
7 join, 8 does

6 1 living, 2 doing, 3 having, 4 having, 5 to work,
6 working, 7 to stay, 8 looking, 9 jogging,
10 to give up, 11 run, 12 getting

7 1 working, 2 not studying, 3 to do, 4 to have,
5 to say

eyg 1 I'm used to it.
2 I'm getting used to the money
3 I wasn't used to working
4 He was used to a busy work schedule.
5 to get used to the time difference

say it *Students' own answers.*

8 1 could, 2 didn't have to, 3 getting,
4 had met, 5 had, 6 had travelled, 7 was,
8 had stayed, 9 not getting, 10 had accepted

9 1 e, 2 d, 3 a, 4 b, 5 c

10 1 f, 2 i, 3 d, 4 a, 5 c, 6 b, 7 g, 8 e

11 1 What do you mean exactly?
2 How come?
3 What's it like?
4 What sort of thing?
5 What for?

say it How come? / What for?
What sort of thing?
What's it like?

eyv 1 g, 2 d / f / i, 3 a / b / e / h
1 flair, 2 pick, 3 at, 4 talented, 5 head, 6 work,
7 uptake, 8 learner

unit two

1 1 That was brave of him.
2 That was kind of him.
3 That was stupid of you.
4 That wasn't very nice of them.
5 That was clever of you.

say it *Students' own answers.*

2 1 d, 2 b, 3 f, 4 a, 5 e

3 1 shouldn't smoke anywhere inside the airport
building.
2 should be here by 10.00.
3 shouldn't have any trouble finding somewhere
to stay.
4 should talk to her as soon as possible and sort
it out.
5 should be 25.
6 should be Kenneth Road, not Tennis Road.
7 shouldn't wear that on the plane. You'll feel
cold.
8 should feel better by tomorrow.

4 1 should've waited (for me).
2 shouldn't have parked (it) there.
3 shouldn't have eaten *so much / such a huge lunch*.
4 should've walked.
5 shouldn't have left *them / the bags* in the car.

say it I should've accepted the offer.
I shouldn't have been late. / I should have
been on time.
He shouldn't have gone to bed so late.

eyv 1 destination, 2 wind down, 3 hectic,
4 make a checklist, 5 essential items,
6 get away, 7 adrenalin rush, 8 recharge,
9 restless, 10 itinerary

5 1 place to get a good map of the area?
2 of getting tickets for tonight's show?
3 get something to eat around here?
4 to buy bus tickets in advance?
5 does it cost to get into the museum?

say it What's the best way to get to the museum?
Do I have to have the correct money for
the bus?
Is there any chance of booking a seat on a
tour for this afternoon?

6 1 a / c, 2 c, 3 b / c, 4 a / c, 5 a / b, 6 a / b / c,
7 a / c, 8 b

7 1 There probably won't be enough.
2 I doubt (if) it'll work.
3 I dare say Fabien will get the job.
4 Things are unlikely to improve.
5 I don't suppose they'll lend me the money.
6 The car's sure to break down.
7 He'll definitely be there.
8 Who's likely to win?

8 1 i, 2 e, 3 h, 4 f, 5 c, 6 a, 7 b, 8 d

eyg 1 have your eyes tested.
2 have them taken up.
3 'm having the car serviced
4 haven't had the phone connected
5 have my jacket dry cleaned.
6 are having their house painted
7 had his bag stolen
8 have it fixed

9 1 It's worth taking a walk along Las Ramblas.
2 I recommend the Picasso Museum.
3 Sitges is worth a visit.
4 You should go and see Figueres.
5 It's worth going to the Miro Museum.

10 1 hostels, 2 breakfast, 3 resort, 4 interest,
5 tour, 6 monuments, 7 trips, 8 charges

unit three

1 1 Do you fancy something to eat?
2 I don't fancy doing that.
3 I don't really fancy the idea of living there.
4 Do you fancy a game of table tennis?
5 I fancy going somewhere different.

say it Do you fancy a coffee?
Do you fancy watching a video?
Do you fancy (going for) a walk?

2 1 compete, 2 relate, 3 consult, 4 get on, 5 hugs,
6 stick, 7 clashed, 8 communicate

3 1 b, 2 c, 3 c, 4 d, 5 b, 6 a, 7 d, 8 c

4 1 *have to / 've got to* pay
2 *mustn't / aren't allowed to* use
3 aren't allowed.
4 're allowed to smoke
5 *have to / 've got to* be
6 don't have to *get / have*
7 *mustn't / aren't allowed to* hang
8 *mustn't / aren't allowed to* repair

say it *Students' own answers.*

eyg 1 need to pay, 2 needs fixing, 3 need mending,
4 need to leave, 5 need to remind

5 1 say, 2 point, 3 makes, 4 right, 5 seems
They are going to try layout 3.

say it Why do you say that?
I don't see the point of that.
That sounds sensible.
That makes sense.

eyv 1 f, 2 g, 3 i, 4 h, 5 a, 6 b, 7 d, 8 e, 9 j, 10 k

say it She's full of life.
He likes to speak his mind.
She's concerned about her appearance.
He's confident and sociable.
She loves to talk.

6 1 e, 2 a, 3 b, 4 d, 5 c

7 1 Set up ten years ago in Holland, the company
is now one of the world's leading software
makers.
2 A very experienced teacher, Gabriella is excited
about taking on the position of headmistress.
3 The son of an architect, Dae-Sang has always
been interested in design.
4 Expanding rapidly, the company now needs
bigger premises.
5 Currently studying languages, Jackie would
like to work as a translator when she finishes
college.

8 1 My alarm clock went off shortly before dawn.
2 Prior to the interview, you should find out as
much as you can about the company.
3 We were friends long before he became famous.
4 They got engaged soon after they met.
5 I feel a lot better since I gave up smoking.

unit four

1 1 surprising, 2 strange, 3 irritating

2 1 g, 2 a, 3 i, 4 b, 5 h, 6 d, 7 f, 8 c

say it *Students' own answers.*

3 1 the end of the day, 2 DVD player,
3 today's paper, 4 make-up artist,
5 husband's boss, 6 bottle opener, 7 night's sleep,
8 house keys

say it the corner of the street
the end of the queue
the beginning of the month

4 1 issue, 2 depends, 3 say

5 1 'll give, 2 'll be playing, 3 won't call,
4 'll have, 5 'll still be working, 6 'll be packing,
7 'll be doing, 8 won't forget

6 1 'll be lying, 2 *'ll be doing / 'll do*, 3 'll give,
4 won't be, 5 'll leave, 6 'll have,
7 'll still be working, 8 Will you get

eyg 1 'll have started
2 Will they have made
3 'll have been
4 'll have found
5 won't have gone

1 'll have met
2 'll be living
3 'll have retired
4 'll probably be doing
5 'll be earning
6 'll have bought
7 'll still be living
8 'll be
9 'll probably *have / have had*
10 'll be working

say it *Students' own answers.*

eyv 1 unemployment, 2 direction, 3 education,
4 communication

1 level of pollution
2 *rate of inflation / inflation rate*
3 sense of achievement
4 standard of education
5 means of transport
6 standard of living
7 sense of direction
8 means of communication

7 1 increase, 2 cut, 3 controlling, 4 examined,
5 will limit, 6 improving, 7 has deteriorated,
8 prohibit

8 1 Do you think you could post this letter for me?
2 Is there any chance you could have a look at
my computer?
3 I was wondering if you could proofread this
report I've written?
4 Do you think you could get some bread on
your way home?
5 Is there any chance you could give me a lift to
the station?

1 b, 2 e, 3 a, 4 f, 5 d

say it *Sample answers*
Is there any chance that you could pick me up
from work tonight?
I was wondering if you could write me a
reference?

9 1 question mark, 2 full stop, 3 tense, 4 paragraph,
5 comma, 6 apostrophe, 7 brackets, 8 hyphen

unit five

1 1 *Ralph / Young Eun*, 2 Tomoko, 3 Ralph, 4 Nina,
5 Alberto

say it *Students' own answers.*

2 1 had already started
2 were you doing
3 were driving
4 hadn't been waiting
5 'd seen
6 was just thinking
7 'd made
8 'd been going out

3 1 believed, 2 had seen, 3 refused, 4 shunted,
5 had applied, 6 was standing,
7 had been waiting, 8 found

4 1 a, 2 a/b/c, 3 c, 4 a/b/c, 5 b/c

5 1 turned up, 2 *'ve failed / failed*, 3 retake,
4 take place, 5 made a mess, 6 didn't come up,
7 *get / got* through, 8 cheating, 9 sit,
10 bluff my way through

6 1 turn … up, 2 get through, 3 going on,
4 turn up, 5 goes on, 6 came up, 7 turned up,
8 get through

7 1 exhausted, 2 Terrifying, 3 fantastic, 4 awful,
5 ridiculous

8 1 *really / fairly*
2 *absolutely / really*
3 *pretty / rather / extremely*
4 *Pretty / Really*
5 *fairly / rather*
6 absolutely
7 *rather / fairly / really*
8 Absolutely

say it *Students' own answers*

9 1 cut off, 2 got rid of, 3 told off, 4 take part in,
5 turned out, 6 takes up, 7 came to an end,
8 work out

eyv 1 e, 2 g, 3 d, 4 k, 5 a, 6 b, 7 j, 8 f, 9 c, 10 h

1 need, 2 find out, 3 asked for, 4 say sorry,
5 put off, 6 let you know, 7 called off,
8 sorted out, 9 get in touch with, 10 get

10 1 It was such a boring film that we walked out
halfway through.
2 The weather was so bad that we decided to
come home early.
3 The test was so difficult that I gave up.
4 It was such disgusting food that I didn't eat
a thing.
5 He got such good results that he decided to
go to college after all.
6 The noise was so loud that I closed the
window.
7 He's such a good teacher that I've decided to
attend his class again next term.
8 The car's so old that I'm not at all surprised it
broke down.

11 1 d, 2 c, 3 a, 4 b, 5 e

eyg 1 … it was much too late to go to the cinema.
2 … looks a little too small for you.
3 I'm way too hungry to wait *for / until* dinner.
4 It'll take far too long to walk there.
5 I'm a bit too tired.
6 … you're way too angry to listen to me.
7 It's slightly too long.
8 It's miles too big for me.

say it *Sample answers*
No, it's a bit too cold for me.
No, it's much too early to leave.
No, it's way too late to start watching a film.

unit six

1 1 d, 2 b, 3 f, 4 a, 5 c

say it You must be ecstatic. / You must be thrilled
to bits. / You must be over the moon.
She must be heartbroken.
He must be really fed up.

2 1 d, 2 a, 3 f, 4 b, 5 c

say it *Students' own answers.*

3 1 surrounding, 2 *badly / seriously*, 3 latest,
4 *seriously / badly*, 5 control, 6 under, 7 fire,
8 terrorist, 9 vitally, 10 extremely

4 1 warning, 2 survival, 3 arrests, 4 injuries,
5 accusations, 6 kidnapping, 7 threat,
8 evacuation

5 1 of, 2 for, 3 at, 4 in, 5 from

6 1 's been arrested, 2 destroyed, 3 were injured,
4 found, 5 hasn't been repaired

7 1 destroyed, 2 were damaged, 3 was robbed,
4 stole, 5 was attacked, 6 attempted,
7 has been won, 8 has been found, 9 claimed,
10 was sentenced

8 1 It seems someone left it in a parked car.
2 Were many people injured?
3 It appears no one was hurt.
4 Did you hear that the school was robbed last
night?
5 Apparently some kids broke in and stole a TV.

eyg 1 She was being followed by a tall man in a
leather jacket.
2 You will be notified of your results next
week.
3 Her house is being painted this week.
4 My credit card had already been used by the
time I reported it stolen.
5 Where is this wine produced?

9 1 have you got a moment?
2 *can / could* you spare a minute?
3 Are you in a hurry?

10 1 if this is the first time you've been to France?
2 how you got here?
3 how long you've been here?
4 if you're by yourself or with a group?
5 if you speak any French?
6 what you think of French food?
7 how you feel about French people?
8 who the President of France is?

say it *Students' own answers.*

11 1 g, 2 f, 3 a, 4 c, 5 b, 6 e, 7 d, 8 i

eyv 1 in depth, 2 on sale, 3 in person, 4 in trouble,
5 on a diet, 6 on purpose, 7 in advance,
8 on the rise, 9 on behalf of, 10 in pain

1 on sale, 2 in advance, 3 on behalf of,
4 in pain, 5 in trouble, 6 in person,
7 on purpose, 8 on the rise, 9 in depth,
10 on a diet

unit seven

1 1 Why on earth didn't you call?
2 Who on earth is that woman?
3 … how on earth will you get home?
4 What on earth have you been doing?
5 Why on earth did she do that?

say it What on earth is that?
What on earth has he been doing?
Why on earth is he dressed like that?

eyg 1 you expected to work at the weekends?
2 were supposed to pick Jane up twenty minutes ago.
3 were expected to do overtime even though we weren't paid for it.
4 're not supposed to take photos in here.
5 'm supposed to go and visit my grandparents on Sunday but I could go on Saturday instead.
6 're not expected to wear a suit and tie but you should look smart.
7 we *expected /supposed* to take a present with us to the party tonight?
8 was supposed to have lunch with Marina but she called it off.

say it I'm expected to write monthly reports.
I'm not expected to work overtime.
I was supposed to go to the meeting yesterday, but I forgot.
I'm not supposed to use the phone for personal calls.

2 1 has he *worked / been working*, 2 's been raining,
3 've been cooking. 4 's called me,
5 've *worn / been wearing*, 6 've read, 7 've burnt,
8 's been staying

3 1 I've never used this computer program …
2 Have you seen any good films recently?
3 Haven't you finished that yet?
4 He's always wanted to be a doctor.
5 I don't think we've met before, have we?

4 1 've always wanted, 2 've just left,
3 haven't worked, 4 've looked after,
5 volunteered, 6 was, 7 really enjoyed,
8 've also *worked / been working*

5 1 I'd be reluctant to work at the weekends.
2 I wouldn't mind doing housework.
3 I'd be prepared to cook meals for the children.
4 I'd find it hard to look after a baby.
5 No, but I'd be willing to get one.

say it *Students' own answers.*

6 1 conservation, 2 raise, 3 charity, 4 donate,
5 fund-raising events

7 1 coping, 2 handle, 3 achieved, 4 a fiasco,
5 succeeded

8 1 endangered, 2 reptiles, 3 captivity, 4 wild,
5 excavate, 6 ruins, 7 bury, 8 site

9 1 those, 2 traffic … seems … doesn't it,
3 advice, 4 outskirts, 5 paper,
6 experience, 7 luggage … is, 8 regards

eyv 1 d, 2 f, 3 e, 4 h, 5 c, 6 b, 7 i, 8 g

1 bunch, 2 spoonfuls, 3 drop, 4 slices, 5 pile,
6 sheet, 7 handful, 8 bundle

10 1 to meet you.
2 I take your jacket?
3 a seat.
4 us OK?
5 any problems getting here?

11 1 Would you need to borrow any money?
2 Sorry, but I won't be able to help.
3 Yeah. Do you need anything?
4 *Will / Would* you give her this book?
5 No, I wouldn't take it.
6 Would you go with them?
7 I'll call you.
8 No thanks, I don't feel hungry.

unit eight

1 1 all over the house 2 all over the world
3 all over her wall 4 all over her hands
5 all over the floor

say it He's got spots all over him.
He's got ink all over his hands.
I've spilt coffee all over my notebook.

2 1 Let go of my bag, or I'll scream.
2 Turn your music down, otherwise I'll call the police.
3 Listen to me, or I won't help you any more.
4 Hurry up, or I'll go without you.
5 Stop looking at my book, otherwise I'll tell the teacher.

3 1 e, 2 d, 3 j, 4 i, 5 h, 6 f, 7 k, 8 a, 9 g, 10 c

4 1 I'm sorry, I didn't do it on purpose.
2 I wasn't aware (that) it was urgent.
3 I didn't realize (that) it belonged to you …
4 I didn't mean to be rude.
5 I didn't realize (that) you were waiting for me.

say it I didn't do it on purpose.
I didn't realize you had guests.
I didn't mean to upset you.

eyg 1 b, 2 c, 3 d, 4 a

1 the noise that I can't stand.
2 I was most unhappy with was the service.
3 that he didn't apologize that made me angry.
4 really annoys me is the fact that he's always late.
5 the waiter's attitude that made things worse.

eyv 1 d, 2 f, 3 i, 4 h, 5 g, 6 c, 7 b, 8 a

1 have a word with you?
2 turn a blind eye to it
3 talk Yumi into helping us.
4 put up with it.
5 talked it over
6 talk them out of complaining?
7 having a go at me.
8 sorted it out.

5 1 threatened, 2 compromise, 3 prove,
4 complaints, 5 reminder, 6 behaviour,
7 suspect, 8 solution

6 1 b / c, 2 a, 3 b, 4 b, 5 a / b, 6 a, 7 c, 8 a / b,
9 a / c, 10 b / c

7 1 *going / that we go*, 2 (that) she still had, 3 to go,
4 her (that) I was married,
5 *not to tell / that I wouldn't tell*, 6 to sack,
7 me to see, 8 *I was harassing / I had harassed*,
9 trying, 10 her to drop

8 1 thinner and thinner
2 *harder and harder / more and more difficult*
3 more and more expensive
4 better and better
5 *faster and faster / quicker and quicker*

say it It's getting worse and worse.
Yes, I'm getting fitter and fitter.
It's getting more and more difficult.

9 1 Despite feeling really sick, she carried on working.
2 I asked to see the manager. However, he wasn't available.
3 *I apologized. He was still angry, though. / Though I apologized, he was still angry.*
4 Despite the spelling mistakes, it was a good essay.
5 Although I told her about it three times, she forgot!
6 He didn't do particularly well in the interview. Nevertheless, I think we should offer him the job.
7 Despite the fact that he had the instructions, he couldn't put it together.
8 In spite of the delay, we arrived on time.

10 1 *In spite of / Despite*, 2 *However / Nevertheless*,
3 *despite / in spite of*, 4 *Despite / In spite* of the fact,
5 although

unit nine

1 1 came out, 2 published, 3 cover, 4 copy,
5 hardback

2 1 I nearly died.
2 I couldn't believe my ears.
3 I nearly fainted.
4 I couldn't believe my eyes.
5 I couldn't believe it.

say it *Students' own answers.*

3 across 1 publicity, 4 slogan, 7 brand, 9 make,
10, invent
down 1 persuade, 2 take, 3 logo, 5 advert,
6 convince, 8 last

4 1 whenever, 2 whichever, 3 however,
4 whatever, 5 whenever, 6 however,
7 Whoever, 8 wherever

say it Whichever you want.
Wherever you want.
Whatever you want.

5 1 is just as good as her last one.
2 is twice as big as my old one.
3 's not nearly as quiet as she used to be.
4 will be nearly as fast as driving at this time of day.
5 's just as well qualified as *him / he is*.
6 isn't nearly as expensive as the Emperor.
7 took twice as long as usual.
8 've done nearly as much work as you!

6 1 The harder … the easier …
2 the longer … the worse …
3 The sooner … the better.
4 The later … the busier …
5 the better … the more money …

7 1 flooding, 2 leaked, 3 depth, 4 wave, 5 stream

8 1 a water-proof camera
2 hand-made chocolates
3 home-grown tomatoes
4 sugar-free gum
5 a multi-purpose tool
6 a mini-dictionary
7 non-toxic paint
8 pre-booked accommodation

9 1 To, 2 So, 3 In case, 4 Otherwise, 5 To

say it So that I could study.
In case it rains.
To have an injection.

eyg 1 account, 2 *due / owing*, 3 because, 4 *As / Since*,
5 *Due / Owing* , 6 *because / on account*, 7 account,
8 *As / Since*

10 1 He's the best player in the team.
2 Who's the most fluent speaker in the class?
3 April is the wettest month of the year in England.
4 She always buys the most expensive thing in the shop.
5 I had the worst time of my life at college last year.

11 1 the tallest man I've ever seen.
2 the most annoying person I've ever met.
3 the most interesting place I've ever been to.
4 the most difficult thing he's ever done.
5 the best film I've seen all year.

say it *Students' own answers.*

eyv 1 f, 2 e, 3 d, 4 a, 5 c

1 breezed in
2 a frosty atmosphere
3 clouded his judgement
4 breezed through the training
5 stormed out

unit ten

1 1 rings a bell, 2 absent-minded,
3 learnt it by heart, 4 mind's gone blank,
5 's on the tip of my tongue

say it *Sample answers*
It's on the tip of my tongue. / My mind's
gone blank.
No, she's very absent-minded.
I learnt it by heart.
I've got a vague memory of it.

2 1 tell he was French? 2 tell the difference,
3 tell one from, 4 tell something was wrong.
5 tell … from

eyv 1 i, 2 a, 3 e, 4 d, 5 g, 6 c, 7 f, 8 h

1 with age, 2 under age, 3 act your age,
4 come of age, 5 look my age, 6 in his old age,
7 over the age of, 8 age limit

3 1 The electric chair was invented by a dentist.
2 Approximately 63,000 trees are used to make
the Sunday edition of the New York Times.
3 Australia is the only continent without reptiles
or snakes.
4 Approximately 50% of the earth is covered
with water.
5 The strongest muscle in the body is the tongue.
6 Neil Armstrong first stepped on the moon with
his right foot.
7 The average adult is 0.4 inches (1cm) taller in
the morning than the evening, because the
spine compresses during the day.
8 The animal responsible for the most deaths in
the world each year is the mosquito.

4 1 The, 2 a, 3 a / the, 4 a, 5 an, 6 the, 7 an, 8
the, 9 the, 10 the / a

5 1 b, 2 a / c, 3 d, 4 f, 5 g

1 immoral, 2 illegal, 3 justifiable, 4 cruel,
5 a shame, 6 inevitable, 7 a nuisance, 8 ridiculous

say it *Students' own answers.*

6 Let me think …
I'll have to think about that for a minute …
That's an interesting question …

say it I've never thought about that before …
That's an interesting question …
Let me think …

7 1 fur, 2 skin, 3 stripes, 4 hunts, 5 herd, 6 beak,
7 spots, 8 stings

8 1 captivity, 2 cruel, 3 justification, 4 sensitivity,
5 constructive, 6 disgraceful, 7 destruction,
8 careless

9 1 –, 2 who, 3 –, 4 which, 5 *that / which*,
6 whose, 7 who, 8 which

10 1 ✓
2 He sold his car, which is the same as mine,
for $5000.
3 ✓
4 ✓
5 His boss, who's a workaholic, insists that
they all work late.
6 Our hotel room, which obviously hadn't
been cleaned for days, was awful.
7 ✓
8 My boss ,who lives in my street, gave me a
lift home.

11 1 , who refused to exchange a pair of shoes I'd
bought the week before.
2 book you gave me to my brother, who lost it.
3 I gave you yesterday was wrong.
4 , who is a lawyer, might be able to help you.
5 know the boy whose bike was stolen?

eyg 1 Fish caught off the north coast is sold in the
cities in the south.
2 The girl going out with my brother is a nurse.
3 The film showing at the moment is new.
4 Their latest record, released two days ago,
has gone straight to the top of the charts.
5 Did you see a man running out of that shop?

1 The man arrested by the police yesterday has
been charged with murder.
2 Do you recognize the man talking to Joe?
3 None of the people interviewed today were
offered the job.
4 The woman walking towards us is Sam's
girlfriend.
5 The diamond stolen from the museum in
1980 has never been recovered.

unit eleven

1 1 a ton, 2 a fortune, 3 a horse, 4 a million years,
5 a hundred times.

say it I could eat a horse.
It weighs a ton.
I wouldn't do that in a million years.
It cost a fortune.

2 1 'd left … wouldn't have missed
2 would have taken … 'd told me
3 'd got … would have seen
4 'd said … wouldn't have told
5 would have been … hadn't left

3 1 wouldn't have finished, 2 'd be working.
3 could've done, 4 would've been, 5 would have

4 1 wouldn't have met
2 *might / would* still be
3 would be
4 wouldn't have been able
5 might still be working
6 *might / would* still be trying
7 *might / would* have gone
8 *might / would* have

5 1 ended up, 2 out of the blue, 3 turned up,
4 by mistake, 5 confide in, 6 put up with,
7 cover … up, 8 ashamed of

eyv 1 mugging, 2 rape, 3 burglary, 4 vandalism,
5 fraud, 6 assault, 7 drug dealing,
8 hooliganism

test yourself vandalism, shoplifting, burglary

6 1 for a while, 2 from you, 3 pleased to hear

7 1 understanding, 2 untrustworthy, 3 unwise,
4 kind-hearted, 5 naive, 6 sincere,
7 open-minded, 8 reckless

eyg 1 it's time you apologized?
2 It's time I went
3 It's time the government did
4 It's time we called
5 It's time I started
6 it's time they gave
7 It's time he retired
8 It's time you took

8 1 b, 2 a, 3 c

say it I'm (*completely / totally*) against it.
I'm (*completely / totally*) in favour of it.
It sounds like an interesting idea.

9 1 f, 2 e, 3 d, 4 g, 5 b, 6 c, 7 a

1 she had to work
2 she was still at
3 she was going to be there until at least
4 she would be too tired
5 I had seen her the night before
6 she had left work for ten minutes
7 he was a colleague
8 I didn't believe her

say it *Students' own answers.*

10 1 It's about, 2 It's all my fault, 3 ring me

unit twelve

1 1 sunrise, 2 dawn … dusk, 3 wide, 4 nap,
5 insomnia, 6 fast, 7 daydreaming, 8 snores

2 1 mean anything to you?
2 doesn't mean anything to him.
3 meant a lot to him.
4 it mean?
5 means a lot to me.

say it What does FR2 mean to you?
Does the name Enrique Alfonso mean
anything to you?
Job satisfaction means a lot to me.

3 1 *if / whether* I was here on holiday.
2 how long I was planning to stay.
3 *if / whether* I knew anyone in the USA.
4 where my aunt lived.
5 where I was going to stay in New York.
6 how much money I had with me.
7 *if / whether* I'd been to the USA before.
8 what I'd done then.

say it She wanted to know if I'd seen Karen
this / that morning.
He asked me why I was late.
She wanted to know where I'd been.
She wanted to know what time I was leaving.

4 1 It's your go next.
2 I think you should go for it.
3 Let me have a go.

5 1 obviously – e
2 *funnily enough / surprisingly* – d
3 *funnily enough / miraculously / luckily /
surprisingly* – g
4 presumably – a
5 *Obviously / Understandably / Presumably* – c
6 Hopefully – i
7 *funnily enough / surprisingly / luckily* – f
8 luckily – b

6 1 gang, 2 jury, 3 pile, 4 choir, 5 crowd, 6 crew,
7 herd, 8 set

test yourself a set of plates
the crew of an aeroplane
a jury

7 1 d, 2 b, 3 e, 4 f, 5 c

8 1 like, 2 like, 3 as, 4 like, 5 like, 6 As, 7 as, 8 as,
9 like, 10 as
You could use *such as* instead of *like* in sentences
2 and 5.

say it He likes spicy food *like / such as* Thai
and Indian.
We had to use my shoe as a hammer.
She looks a bit like Gwyneth Paltrow.
He's just started work as a teacher.

eyv 1 a mental task, 2 maximize, 3 focus,
4 visualizing, 5 functioning, 6 stimulating,
7 have sth on your mind, 8 distractions

1 visualize, 2 function, 3 stimulating, 4 focus,
5 have something on my mind, 6 distractions,
7 maximize, 8 clear my head

9 1 straightforward, 2 hang, 3 complicated,
4 follow, 5 simple

10 1 compete, 2 throws, 3 win, 4 miss, 5 take, 6 is,
7 guess, 8 give

eyg 1 what he'll say
2 why I'm so tired.
3 what time the film starts.
4 where we are.
5 if Judy wants to come with us.
6 where Mayumi's gone.
7 how long it'll take
8 where I put my keys.

OXFORD
UNIVERSITY PRESS

Great Clarendon Street, Oxford OX2 6DP

Oxford University Press is a department of the University of Oxford. It furthers the University's objective of excellence in research, scholarship, and education by publishing worldwide in

Oxford New York

Auckland Bangkok Buenos Aires Cape Town Chennai Dar es Salaam Delhi Hong Kong Istanbul Karachi Kolkata Kuala Lumpur Madrid Melbourne Mexico City Mumbai Nairobi São Paulo Shanghai Taipei Tokyo Toronto

Oxford and Oxford English are registered trade marks of Oxford University Press in the UK and in certain other countries

© Oxford University Press 2003

The moral rights of the author have been asserted

Database right Oxford University Press (maker)

First published 2003
Second impression 2003

ISBN 0 19 437333 9

Designed by Bryony Newhouse

Printed in China

Acknowledgements

The Publisher and Authors are grateful to the following for permission to reprint copyright material:

p.29 'When push comes to shove in High Street' by Alan Hamilton © Times Newspapers Limited 19 July 2001. Reproduced by permission.

Although every effort has been made to trace and contact copyright holders before publication, this has not been possible in some cases. We apologize for any apparent infringement of copyright and if notified, the publisher will be pleased to rectify any errors or omissions at the earliest opportunity.

Illustrations

Cyrus Deboo pp.19, 54; Mark Draisey p.11; Martina Farrow pp.16, 33, 35, 46; Phil Healey pp.7, 55, 72; Pamela Hobbs pp.23, 37, 40, 60 (snake, earth, astronaut, mosquito), 67, 73; Roger Penwill pp 59, 63; Gavin Reece pp.4, 10, 30, 56, 60 (girl under tree), 69; Harry Venning p.22.

Picture research by:
Mark Ruffle

The Publisher and Authors would like to thank the following for their kind permission to reproduce photographs:

Corbis pp.15 (D. S. Robbins), 66 (M. Prince / woman, S. Chenn / couple); Corbis royalty free p.6 (high jump); Corel pp.12 (beach); Getty images: cover, p.1 (Uwe Krejci / 2 people); Image Bank p.39 (Sparky); Network Photographers p.52 (M. Mayer); Photodisc pp.6 (footballers, mountain bikers, tennis), 12 (castle, rafting), 20 (Clara, Carlos, Martin, Felix, Pierre), 42, 66 (man), and all circular and square icon images throughout; Rex Features p.21; Stockbyte p.65; Stone pp.8 (T. Doyle), 13 (J. Riley), 17 (L. Adamski Peek), 24 (D. Roth), 25 (F. Thatcher), 35 (A. Weinbrecht), 45 (B. Ayres), 50 (C. Bissell), 53 (S. Krouglikoff / woman, T. Flach / man, R. Krisel / man), 64 (E. Dreyer); Taxi pp.18 (S. Rausser), 28 (L. Delhourne), 70 (J. P. Fruchet), 71 (V.C.L.); WWF-UK p.43 (www.panda.org/www.wwf.org.uk/logo).

The Publisher and Authors would like to thank Louise Williams for her report on the manuscript of this workbook.